LONDON UNDERGROUND ROLLING STOCK

BRIAN HARDY

Capital Transport

First published 1976
Twelfth edition 1990

ISBN 185414 130 9

Published by Capital Transport Publishing
38 Long Elmes, Harrow Weald, Middlesex

Printed by Hastings Printing Company, Hastings, Sussex

© Capital Transport Publishing and Brian Hardy 1990

AUTHOR'S NOTE

This book describes and illustrates each type of rolling stock on London's Underground railway system with information on changes and developments since the last edition was published. Since the previous edition, extensive changes have been made to London Underground's management structure, giving the ten lines their own separate identity. The former Hammersmith & City and Circle sections of the Metropolitan Line are now lines in their own right (albeit managed as one Circle & Hammersmith Line) as is the East London Line. It should be appreciated, of course, that a certain amount of interworking must continue to exist, especially with the Metropolitan and Circle/Hammersmith.

Over the years, many changes have taken place in the allocation and types of stock running on the different lines. The numbers of passengers using the Underground had fallen to an all-time low of 498 million in 1982, at which time services and rolling stock requirements were tailored to suit. With the introduction of a zoned fares structure and the Travelcard, passenger usage dramatically increased, setting an all-time high record of 815 million passengers in the year 1988-89 (a decrease to 765 million in 1989-90). This required more rolling stock very quickly and saw five trains of 1938 Tube Stock (which had been withdrawn) return to service on the Northern Line between September 1986 and May 1988. Some of these stalwarts can now be found on the Isle of Wight — fit for another 15 years service!

Although this book is not an official publication of London Underground Ltd, the Author expresses his thanks to the London Underground Press Office, the Principal Rolling Stock Engineer and his staff and to friend and colleague Bob Greenaway for his guidance and help, especially with the selection of photographs. A special note of thanks also goes to Piers Connor and Oliver Fried, particularly with the more technical matters, and to Jacqueline Hardy for checking the typescript. The writer would also like to record his thanks to Mr B. Quinn, head of Mail Rail, and to Derek Varrier for assistance given on the Post Office Railway, and to Chris Bennett for information on the Docklands Light Railway.

In order to keep the information in this book up to date, regular rolling stock information is published in the London Underground Railway Society's monthly news magazine, 'Underground News'.

BRIAN HARDY

The diagrams of car layouts are by Mike Harris

CONTENTS

Front Cover A train of 1959 stock, painted in Standard stock livery as part of the commemoration of the centenary of electric tube railways in 1990. It is seen at Finchley Central. *R.J. Greenaway*

Front Cover Lower Painted 1972 stock in three different liveries can be seen on the Northern Line. The paint scheme decided on for the main programme of refurbishments is illustrated in this view at Hendon. *LUL/Northern Line*

A six-car train of C stock at West Brompton on the District Line Wimbledon–Edgware Road service.
C.D. Jones

All C69 and C77 stock is to be refurbished by RFS Engineering of Doncaster. C69 DM 5543 is seen on
the M1 motorway near the M25 junction on 26th May 1990 heading for Doncaster. R.J. Greenaway

Top **Fully refurbished A62 stock unit 5132, in the livery to be adopted for future painting of aluminium passenger stock, approaches Wembley Park.** F.W. Ivey

Redundant through the 1967/72 stock additional trains programme, UNDM 3429 has been used in experiments with liveries and interior decor schemes for 1972 stock refurbishment. It is seen in Acton Works sporting two different liveries, neither of which has been adopted. R.J. Greenaway

INTRODUCTION

London Underground Ltd operates two main types of rolling stock on its railways. One is known as surface stock and is built to full-size gauge for use on the Metropolitan, Circle and District Lines whose tunnel sections are double-tracked and built just below surface level. The other type, tube stock, is used on the Bakerloo, Piccadilly, Northern, Jubilee, Central and Victoria Lines, which have deep-level single-track tube tunnels of about 12ft diameter.

In the case of tube stock the different groups are distinguished by the year of anticipated delivery at the time of ordering. Surface stock is distinguished by letters and the last two digits of the year of anticipated delivery. The District Line stock, now officially known as plain D stock, was originally designated D78 stock.

Each train is composed of one or more units coupled as necessary to form trains of required length. Units are formed of a number of motor cars and trailer cars semi-permanently coupled. Each unit is self-sufficient as regards current supply for motors, lighting, compressed air supply and auxiliary equipment. Some stocks have units which cannot be operated on their own as they have a driver's cab at one end only.

The different types of car are:

DM   Driving Motor car, having traction motors and a driver's cab.
NDM   Non-Driving Motor car; as DM but without a driver's cab.
UNDM Uncoupling Non-Driving Motor car; as NDM but provided with control cabinet at one end to allow uncoupling and shunting of a unit without loss of space incurred by full-size cab.
T   Trailer car; without motors or cab.

To assist in identification, the end cars of units are referred to as 'A' cars (which normally face north or west) or 'D' cars (south or east). Car numbering is arranged so that distinction can not only be made between 'A' and 'D' cars, but also between the types of car and stock. It should be pointed out, however, that with the existence of loop lines (Kennington, Northern Line, and Heathrow, Piccadilly Line), trains on these lines will become 'turned' and may face the opposite direction to that mentioned above.

The manifestation of London Underground's policy of extending one-person operation to tube lines was achieved on the Piccadilly Line on 31st August 1987, the 1973 stock having been converted at Northfields depot and Acton Works. OPO on the Jubilee Line commenced on 28th March 1988, the first batch of 1983 stock having been converted at Acton Works, while the 1983 (batch II) was delivered in converted form. The 1972 MkII stock was also modified at Acton Works so that OPO on the Bakerloo Line was achieved on 20th November 1989. This leaves the Central and Northern Lines crew-operated, but OPO is envisaged when the replacement stock is delivered for those lines. At present this is anticipated from March 1992 for the Central Line, when the first of the new trains is expected to enter service.

The oldest of the surface stock is the A60/62 stock on the Metropolitan main line, which was converted to one-person operation during 1985-86. OPO was introduced on 29th September 1986, the Metropolitan being the last of the 'surface' lines of the Underground to be so converted. The A60 stock can also be found on the East London Line, sufficient units being available after the conversions to one-person operation had been completed.

In order to reduce costs and improve efficiency, the heavy overhaul of trains has been taken away from Acton Works and transferred to selected rolling stock depots. The first depot to undertake this role was Golders Green in September 1985, followed by Stonebridge Park, Cockfosters, Northumberland Park and Upminster in 1986. Neasden followed suit in 1987, and Ruislip also commenced interior refurbishing work on 1962 stock in the same year. Ealing Common started overhauling D stock in 1988 and in the following year full overhauls commenced at Ruislip on the 1962 stock.

Interior of the lifting shop in Ruislip depot. Ruislip, along with some other depots, is performing overhauls in lieu of a centralised location for such work.
Capital Transport

Since the creation of the Line Business Units, some of the Underground lines have sought to make their identity on rolling stock. An example is seen on 1983 (batch I) Tube Stock at Canons Park, with the Jubilee Line name affixed beside the cab door of DM 3728. Unit 3663 of batch II also has the line name.
R.J. Waterhouse

The line allocations of the different types of stock, including spares, are shown below as at 30th September 1990.

Bakerloo Line	1972 MkII stock	33	trains
Jubilee Line	1983 stock (batch I)	15	trains
	1983 stock (batch II)	16½	trains
Central Line	1960 stock	3	trains
	1962 stock	84	trains*
Northern Line	1956 stock	3	trains
	1959 stock	75	trains*
	1962 stock	2½	trains
	1972 MkI stock	25½	trains*
Piccadilly Line	1973 stock	87½	trains*
Victoria Line	1967 stock	39½	trains*
	1967/72 stock (converted)	3½	trains
District Line	C69/77 stock	11	trains‡
	D stock	75	trains*
East London Line	A60 stock	7	units†
H&C and Circle Lines	C69/77 stock	35	trains*
Metropolitan Line	A60/62 stock	53½	trains*

* Includes withdrawn or damaged stock extant.
† Single four-car units operate on this line
‡Wimbledon–Edgware Road section.

Close up of a 1959 stock at Morden recently overhauled, showing the Underground roundel, Northern Line name and new signwork. The interiors are now being painted in cream as seen here.
Capital Transport

Q38 pilot motors 4416/7 and Q35 trailer 08063 pass through Earl's Court on 2nd August 1990 on their way to Upminster depot for the open day.
F.W. Ivey

Battery locomotive L44 was repainted in July 1990 with green sides, and is seen passing Dagenham Heathway on 5th August 1990 hauling two BR coaches on loan to LUL, and Metropolitan steam locomotive No. 1.
R.J. Greenaway

A between-cars view of NDM 9601 and DM 1601 showing the Central Line name now applied to all Central Line 1962 stock. The only visible difference between 1962 stock NDMs and DMs and the 1959 stock is the join line above the car numbers of the former. Note also that the grab rails have been removed.
Capital Transport

SUMMARY OF CARS OWNED

	For Service*				Special Duties and Withdrawn Stock				Total Cars
	DM	NDM	UNDM	T	DM	NDM	UNDM	T	
Tube Stock									
1938					2	1		1	4
1956	12	3		6					21
1959	300	75		150					525
1960	6			3					9
1962†	346	170		173	1	2			692
1967‡	172			172					344
1972 MkI	76		26	76			4		182
1972 MkII	99		33	99					231
1973	195		153	174	1		1		524
1983 batch I	60			30					90
1983 batch II	66			33					99
1986					6	6			12
Total Tube:	1332	248	212	916	10	9	5	1	2733
Surface Stock									
A60	122			122				2	246
A62	106			106				1	213
C69	106			106					212
C77	33			33					66
D	170		130	150					450
Total Surface:	537		130	517				3	1187
Grand Total:	1869	248	342	1433	10	9	5	4	**3920**

Notes: *Includes damaged and stored stock likely to be returned to service.
†Includes NDMs built in 1959 to run with the Central Line 1962 Tube Stock.
‡Includes conversions from 1972 MkI Tube Stock.

The appearance of the 1956 Tube Stock changed considerably in 1990 when the original five headcode lights were replaced by powerful twin headlights. Birmingham built DM 1007 is at the rear of a southbound Northern Line train departing from Camden Town. A Golders Green 'GG' overhaul logo is carried to the left of the new headlights. Capital Transport

Facing Page **Gloucester built 1956 stock arrives at Euston on the southbound City branch of the Northern Line, showing that the Gloucester units have a beading line at waist level and straight rainstrips over the passenger doors.** Capital Transport

When the pre-1938 stock on the Piccadilly Line was becoming due for replacement, three prototype trains were ordered in anticipation of a large order for new stock. Metro-Cammell, the Birmingham Railway Carriage & Wagon Company and the Gloucester Railway Carriage & Wagon Company each built a prototype train formed into seven cars comprising a semi-permanently coupled three- and four-car unit (M-T-NDM-M+M-T-M).

Although very much an updated version of the 1938 tube stock, the trains, known as 1956 stock, were finished in unpainted aluminium for the exterior, and the interior paintwork was blue. In recent years the original grey, red and black seating moquette has been replaced by blue. Fluorescent lighting was used for the first time on tube stock (following an experiment on 1938 stock DM car 11294 from late-1953), twin tubes running at intervals the whole length of the car in the centre of the ceiling. In order to reduce the number of wearing parts, rubber suspension was provided on the car bogies.

The seating capacity is similar to that on the 1938 stock, but the transverse seats in the centre bay were rearranged in facing pairs. A main distinguishing feature of the interiors

compared with the 1959 stock which followed, is the use of deeper cushions similar to those on 1938 stock. No tip-up seats are fitted at the car ends for passengers, but one tip-up seat (lockable when not in use) is provided at the guard's position on DM cars. A roller destination blind illuminated by a fluorescent tube from behind is provided above the centre cab door on the motor cars, and external door-indicator lights are fitted.

When originally delivered, the two middle driving motor cars only of each train were fitted with Wedglock automatic couplers, the driving motor cars at the outer ends being fitted with mechanical couplers. These trains entered service on the Piccadilly Line during 1957 and 1958 and were the forerunners of a large order of similar 1959 tube stock.

In order to operate with 1959 stock, the three prototype trains were later equipped with Wedglock automatic couplers on the driving motor cars at the leading ends. All 1956 stock cars were renumbered in 1965 to conform with the 1959 stock.

The 1956 stock was transferred from the Piccadilly Line to the Northern Line during 1976 and 1977, on which line it operates today, being fully compatible with the 1959 stock.

During July 1990 the three trains of 1956 stock were modified at Highgate depot, where a 'passenger alarm' system and public address equipment were installed as part of many safety measures to update and improve rolling stock. The passenger alarm system (which has been fitted to all new stock from 1973 onwards) replaces the passenger emergency pull-down handles, which immediately stop a train when operated. The new system alerts the driver, but allows the train to be driven to the next station, where the problem can be more easily dealt with. A further modification made at the same time was that the five headlights on each driving motor car were replaced by powerful twin headlights, considerably altering the frontal appearance for the first time since the trains were new.

Newly overhauled unit 1056 arrives at Finchley Central. This unit was the prototype for the safety modifications programme, having been completed in July 1989. Recently overhauled units have had new style signs and car numbers, along with the Northern Line 'logo' of the archer. Unfortunately no overhauled units on the Northern Line have yet had their roof appearance improved. Capital Transport

Following successful trials with the 1956 prototype stock, orders were placed with Metro-Cammell for 76 seven-car trains to replace the same number of pre-1938 stock trains on the Piccadilly Line. The 15 trains of 1938 stock then in service on the Piccadilly Line were to continue to operate on the line for the time being.

The 76 new trains were virtually identical to the 1956 stock, but included automatic couplers on all driving motor cars and twin headlights replaced the five marker lights of the 1956 cars, as headcodes were being phased out. The first train entered service on 14th December 1959. Driving motor cars were numbered 1012 onwards ('A' end even numbers and 'D' end odd numbers), trailers from 2012 and every even number onwards, and non-driving motor cars from 9013 and every alternate odd number onwards.

While the 1959 stock was being delivered there was a change of plan regarding the replacement of Central Line standard stock. The original idea was to design a new type of rolling stock for this, but as there was insufficient time owing to the expected increase in passenger traffic from the Eastern Region suburban electrification into Liverpool Street, it was decided to deliver the last 57 trains of 1959 stock to the Central Line. Each Central Line train formation is made up of eight cars, and therefore an additional 57 non-driving motor cars were ordered from Metro-Cammell in order to lengthen the 57 trains to eight cars, formed of two four-car units (M-T-NDM-M+M-T-NDM-M). The first eight-car train of 1959 stock entered service on the Central Line on 25th July 1960, although two seven-car trains had been at work on the line during March and April for crew training purposes.

At the same time, orders were placed with the Birmingham Railway Carriage & Wagon Company for 338 driving motor cars and 112 non-driving motor cars, and with the BR workshops at Derby for 169 trailers. As Birmingham were unable to fulfil their contract, their order was transferred to Metro-Cammell. This stock for the Central Line was designated 1962 stock, but deliveries continued without interruption when the 1959 stock was completed. The two stocks are almost identical in appearance and design, and despite slight variations in equipment, are interchangeable in service. The numbers of 1962 stock motor cars started at 1400, trailers at 2400 and non-driving motor cars at 9401. The first train of 1962 stock entered service on 12th April of that year.

The delivery of 1962 tube stock allowed the 1959 stock to be returned to the Piccadilly Line less the 57 additional non-driving motor cars, which were reformed into the 1962 tube stock. These had been numbered from the start in the Central Line 1962 stock series. All 1959 stock had been transferred to the Piccadilly Line by mid-1964.

Three additional eight-car trains and one additional three-car train of 1962 stock were ordered and delivery followed on from the main batch of 1962 stock. The eight-car trains were required to replace the same number of 1960 prototype stock trains then on the Central Line which were required for trials with Automatic Train Operation. The additional three-car unit was destined for the Piccadilly Line Holborn-Aldwych shuttle.

Over the years a number of modifications and experiments have been conducted on the 1959 and 1962 stocks. Some of these will now be described:

A seven-car train (1020-2020-9021-1021+1022-2022-1023) was fitted with electrically-operated door equipment in 1963 in place of the usual air-operated equipment. The train lasted in this form until 1977 (1022-2022-1023) and 1978 (1020-2020-9021-1021) when the units reverted to standard door operation on their impending transfer to the Northern Line.

Thirty trailers of 1959 stock and 25 trailers of 1962 stock are fitted with de-icing equipment, enabling fluid from a special tank under the car to be spread onto the current rails to prevent ice forming. In addition, small brushes can be lowered to sweep the current rails clear of snow. The equipment is controlled by switches in the driver's cab. Such cars are identified by having a letter 'D' under the car number.

In September 1973 trailer 2020 had its roof painted silver and NDM 9021 white, in an experiment aimed at reducing the temperature inside the cars in hot weather.

In 1974 NDM 9153 was fitted with heavy-duty fire-resistant carpet in place of the traditional maple wood flooring. The carpet wore well but the experiment did not meet favourably with the travelling public and it was removed in October 1978.

Interior of a 1959 Tube Stock driving motor car at Edgware. Amongst the safety modifications made during 1989/90 was the installation of public address equipment and passenger alarm buttons, as seen over the open door on the left. R.A. Ashman

1962 stock NDM 9629 has been fitted with external door inspection hatches at floor level to allow easier access to the door tracks.

Three 1959 stock trailer cars are equipped with thermostatically-controlled car heaters, each of a different type: 2036 (GEC), 2054 (English Electric) and 2110 (AEI).

Stabling lights have been fitted to 1959 and 1962 stock DMs, but owing to the slightly different cab layouts between the two types of stock, they are located on opposite sides of the twin headlights.

During July 1979, 1962 stock DMs 1442 and 1445 were given half-red painted cab ends like the 1973 stock, for visibility tests. The train initially worked as a 'block' eight-car formation but was later split up. DM 1445 reverted to normal in November 1982 and 1422 in February 1983.

1962 stock trailer 2608 (which was renumbered 2692 in 1983) has experimental 'Permatread' car flooring.

The outer driving cabs of 1959 stock have been fitted with train radio for two-way communication between the driver and line controller, a modification which has also been made to the other trains of 1959/62 stock on the Northern Line and similarly on the Central Line's 1962 stock. On the Central Line, however, there are a number of four-car units with train radio fitted at each end, as four-car units are operated on their own on the shuttle services.

A westbound Central Line train of 1962 Tube Stock arrives at Tottenham Court Road. Leading is DM 1580 of a double-ended four-car unit, as illustrated by the receptacle box. On single-ended units this equipment is confined to the middle DMs. Note that the car number is located at cantrail height on overhauled units. Capital Transport

Although the 1959 stock was always associated with the Piccadilly Line and the 1962 stock with the Central Line, there has been a small number of occasions when stock from one line has worked on the other for various reasons, albeit for generally short periods of time. Two 1959 stock cars, DM 1071 and trailer 2070, were scrapped in 1973 and 1974 respectively following a collision at Uxbridge. The spare DM remaining (1070) was reformed into various 1962 stock units which had a west-end DM car out of use awaiting repair. DM car 1309 was damaged beyond repair by a bomb explosion at Wood Green in March 1976. Its place was later taken by 1070. As 1070 was an 'A' end car it was converted to a 'D' end car, turned and renumbered 1309R in August 1977. It returned to service on the Piccadilly Line in September very briefly, and was transferred to the Northern Line in October 1977. The original 1309 was scrapped in December 1977. Three cars, 1052, 2052 and 9053 were scrapped as a result of a collision near Kensal Green on 16th October 1986 when a class 313 EMU ran into a southbound Bakerloo Line train halted at signals. The three cars were replaced respectively by 1084, 2084 and 9085, which had become spare from March 1985 as a result of 1959 stock overhaul work being done at Golders Green depot. The odd car remaining, 1085, replaced 1031 following the latter's damage beyond repair in 1986. DM 1085 was renumbered 1031R.

The commissioning of 1973 tube stock for the Piccadilly Line started in 1975, allowing 1959 stock to be transferred to the Northern Line. These transfers started in November

A westbound Central Line train arrives at Oxford Circus. Note that the leading DM is 'D' end, as confirmed by the location of the receptacle box under the driver's window. Note also that the side grab rails have been removed following their abuse by the hooligan element of society. Capital Transport

1975 and the last took place on 12th October 1979. The last train of 1959/62 stock in service on the Piccadilly Line (main) was 1728-2728-9729-1729+1218-2218-1219 on Friday 5th October 1979. The last 1962 stock train to operate on the Aldwych branch was 1750-2750-1751 on Wednesday 17th October 1979, and on the following day 1973 stock took over the service. Unit 1750-2750-1751 was subsequently transferred to the Northern Line, where it operated with the 1959 tube stock until transferred to the Central Line in 1989.

With the additional amount of rolling stock made available by the December 1982 service reductions, fifteen trains of 1959 tube stock were transferred to the Bakerloo Line from the Northern Line. The first train to be transferred for rolling stock staff training was moved on 5th December 1982 (units 1212 and 1203), the last train being received at Stonebridge Park depot on 3rd October 1983 (units 1216 and 1223). Fourteen trains of 1938 tube stock were thus withdrawn for scrapping. The outer driving cabs of 1959 stock have been fitted with train radio for two-way communication between the driver and line controller, a modification which has also been made to the other trains of 1959/62 stock on the Northern Line. The first train of 1959 tube stock entered service on the Bakerloo Line on 28th February 1983. One extra train of 1959 stock was transferred from the Northern to the Bakerloo on 25th January 1984 to provide the one extra train required for the Harrow & Wealdstone service, which was restored in peak hours from 4th June 1984. To make up the stock required for the Northern Line, three trains of 1962 stock were transferred from the Central Line, each train less one NDM car because the former operates only seven-car trains.

The new 1983 stock for the Jubilee Line allowed trains of 1972 MkII stock to be transferred to the Northern Line and more trains of 1959 stock from the Northern to the Bakerloo, which saw the end (for the time being) of the 1938 stock on 20th November 1985. The last transfer of 1959 stock to the Bakerloo was achieved the following day.

With the need to increase services and to start the first phase of OPO conversion of 1972 MkII stock, 13 trains of 1959 stock were returned to the Northern Line in exchange for the same number of 1972 MkII trains between May and September 1986. The outstanding 18 trains of 1959 stock are being returned to the Northern Line now that the 1983 (batch II) stock is entering service, allowing the 1972 MkII stock currently on the Jubilee Line to be transferred to the Bakerloo. The last train of 1959 stock left the Bakerloo for the Northern Line on 7th July 1989, from which date all 1959 stock trains were back on the Northern.

Until 1989 the 1962 stock fleet was still complete insofar as numbers originally delivered. However, a number of vehicles had been stored for some years as the result of various collisions and the surplus cars were disposed of during 1989 and 1990. These were: five DM cars, 1458, 1459 (originally 1501), 1542, 1658 and 1733; three NDM cars, 9733, 9741 (originally 9657) and 9749; and three trailers, 2458, 2542 and 2658. NDM 9543 continues to be stored out of service at Hainault depot. Spare NDM 9659 was renumbered 9751 in 1989 when three-car unit 1750-2750-1751 was transferred from the Northern to the Central, enabling the unit to be lengthened from three to four cars.

In addition to the 1962 stock trailers renumbered during 'half-life' overhauls (listed later in the book), other cars have been renumbered as follows because of collision reformations: 9741 was renumbered 9657 to replace the original which was damaged, 9459 and 1459 were renumbered 9501 and 1501 respectively (the original 1501 was renumbered 1459 and scrapped, while the original 9501 survives as a Sandite car but renumbered 9459). DM 1659 was renumbered to 1531 to replace the original, while the original 1531 was subsequently repaired and took the place of 1416 (having to be converted from a 'D' end DM to an 'A' end DM). The original 1416 is awaiting disposal.

In 1989 a programme was started to improve the safety features of both 1959 and 1962 stocks. This included installing 'passenger alarm' and public address equipment. The 1959 stock work (plus the Northern Line's 2½ trains of 1962 stock, and one train from the Central Line) was undertaken at Highgate depot by TB Precision of Tipton, while the 1962 stock modifications were done by BREL at their Derby and Crewe works.

To celebrate 100 years of electric tube railways, of which the Northern Line section between Borough and Stockwell is part of the original City & South London Railway, one train of 1959 stock has been painted into 1923 style livery. This comprises Underground train red with maroon doors, grey roof, cream around the saloon windows and around the trailing ends of the cars, and black lining. The interior has also been painted cerulean blue (which actually looks 'green') and upholstery is in 1920s style. The painting work was done by Vic Berry of Leicester and the train re-entered service in its new guise on 19th July 1990 (units 1044 and 1031).

The Northern Line's seven-car 'Heritage' train of 1959 stock was 'launched' in July 1990 and is seen with DM 1031 at the front at Edgware.
F.W. Ivey

The interiors of the 'Heritage' cars have also been treated in 1920s fashion, including period-style moquette.
LUL

Former 1962 stock NDM 9501 was converted to become a 'Sandite' rail treatment car in 1989, and has been renumbered 9459. It was repainted into this three-tone red/white/blue livery in 1990, as seen here in Ealing Common depot.
David Rowe

Still in original unpainted aluminium condition, DM 3903 of 1960 Tube Stock arrives at Hainault on a shuttle working from Woodford. The other two three-car units have now been painted in 1938 stock livery. P.M. Bradley

In preparation for the replacement of the Central Line's pre-1938 tube stock, 12 new experimental motor cars were ordered from Cravens Ltd, Sheffield. These were formed into six four-car units using 12 trailer cars converted from existing pre-1938 stock trailers (M-T-T-M). The original plan was to test these units thoroughly in passenger service on the Central Line in eight-car formations before deciding on the final type of replacement stock for that line.

As described in the previous chapter, it became necessary to re-equip the Central Line with new stock earlier than anticipated. Also, the pre-1938 stock was very expensive to convert for use with new motor cars. The plan to order a further 338 new driving motor cars and convert a further 338 pre-1938 stock trailers after the testing of the prototype units was therefore abandoned in favour of the 1959 stock design currently being delivered.

Like the 1959 stock, the 1960 prototype stock was finished in unpainted aluminium and fluorescent lighting was fitted inside. The main visible differences were the six double-width windows on each side of the cars, casement windows of the same size inside the cars giving a double glazing effect, and the redesigned cab ends. Car ventilators were provided above the casement windows, being pulled downwards to open, and each ventilator frame was long enough to accommodate the Central Line diagram. The draught screens by the doors were set back further than on previous stock to allow quicker boarding and alighting when passengers were standing by the doors. The seating capacity of each driving motor car was reduced to 40 as compared to 42 on the 1959/62 stock DMs. Experimental blue/pink or green/yellow and blue interior liveries were tried out on the cars.

An improved type of automatic Wedglock coupler was introduced on the motor cars. Unlike previous stock where an 'A' end motor could only be coupled to a 'D' end motor and vice versa, these cars could be coupled additionally 'A' end to 'A' end and 'D' end to 'D' end. This was achieved by duplicating the electrical connections through the coupler.

The driving motor cars were numbered 3900 to 3911 and the 12 converted trailers were renumbered 4900 to 4911. This numbering replaced an original plan to number the motor cars from 3000 and the converted trailers from 4000, which would have come into being if the 338 driving motor cars had been built and 338 trailers converted. The first two motor cars, 3900 and 3901, were in fact numbered 3000 and 3001 by Cravens and were renumbered 3900 and 3901 after delivery to Ruislip depot.

The conversion work on the trailers at Acton Works included the fitting of fluorescent lighting inside the cars, provision of external door-indicator lights and the painting of the outside silver to match the unpainted driving motor cars. Of the 12 converted trailers four were of 1927 vintage, two of which were rebuilt with additional end single doors. The other eight cars were built in 1931 by Birmingham and Gloucester. The 1960 stock first entered service on the Central Line in November 1960 in eight-car formation (M-T-T-M + M-T-T-M).

In 1964, in anticipation of providing fully automatic trains for the Victoria Line, following the success on District Line tracks of Automatic Train Operation (ATO) on a limited scale, it was decided to use the Central Line's Hainault-Woodford branch for further trials. Acton Works converted five four-car units of 1960 stock for this purpose, the remaining unit being kept for engineering tests. The most visible alterations were the 'blocking up' of the side cab doors, pull-down windows being provided in their place. The only access was via the door in the passenger car or the front cab door. The set number plates were relocated in the front cab door and the position of the tripcock resetting cord was altered so that it could be reset from the front cab without the operator having to climb down onto the track. Door controls were re-located in the driving cabs. ATO started on the Hainault-Woodford branch in April 1964 and provided the testing ground for the Victoria Line 1967 stock on delivery.

Four-car unit 3904-4904-4905-3905 had its passenger emergency handles replaced by key resettable push buttons. This system incorporated an electrical circuit around the train, which when broken by the pushing of an emergency button causes an emergency application of the brakes. The system also eliminated the need for a second air pipe along the train, and having proved successful was incorporated in 1973 stock.

The four-car unit not converted for ATO (3910-4902-4903-3911), but used for engineering tests, was transferred to the service stock fleet in 1971. It was used as a 'track recording train' until mid-1977, when the unit entered Acton Works for overhaul of the DMs.

With the converted pre-1938 stock trailers being almost 50 years old, replacement by spare trailers of 1938 tube stock was commenced. No.4929 (ex-012392) was completed in February 1976 and replaced 4908/9, which were withdrawn in November 1975 when DMs 3908/9 entered Acton Works for overhaul. DMs 3908/9 were given black painted car roofs, stabling lights on the driving ends and sleet brushes on the leading bogies. The interiors of the overhauled motor cars and newly converted trailer were painted blue.

The second car to be converted was 4927 (ex-012229) in April 1977 and replaced 4906/7 which were scrapped in August 1977. The two DMs (3906/7) were treated in the same way as the first overhauled pair, except that the car roofs were painted grey. However, at this time it was discovered that DMs 3906 to 3911 had asbestos and they were immediately withdrawn for decontamination. Converted cars 4927/9 were stored, while the trailers from 3910/1 (4902/3) were scrapped. By April 1978, a further two trailers had been converted; 4921 (ex-012366) and TRC912 (ex-012331), the latter car being converted to replace 4902/3 in the Track Recording Train, but these were also placed in store.

In September 1980 trailers 4921/7 were transferred to Hainault from store at Acton, pending the completion of the work on 3906-9. The first pair (3906/7) were transferred back to Hainault on 30th November 1980, with 3908/9 following on 22nd March 1981. It was intended that 3910/1 should have been completed also, but these cars have now been scrapped and the converted trailer (TRC912) was stored in Acton Works. It is now a stores vehicle at Ealing Common.

The four trailers of converted Pre-1938 tube stock that remained in 1980 (4900/1/4/5) were given a minor internal refurbishment in September 1980 (4904/5) and early 1981 (4900/1) with new seating and interior blue paintwork. The exteriors were also repainted, but in white rather than silver as previously. However, the four trailers were withdrawn in 1982 and scrapped in August 1983, the four DMs (3900/1/4/5) being stored at Hainault. DMs 3901 and 3905 were subsequently selected to become pilot motor cars for the Underground's track recording vehicle, and were transferred from Hainault to Ruislip on 29th June 1986. From Ruislip they were despatched by road to BREL Derby on 10th July, where they were converted. The two DMs were renumbered L132 and L133.

DM 3906 of 1960 stock, painted in 1938 stock livery, enters Epping whilst working the Ongar shuttle on the 27th May 1990. R.J. Greenaway

With the original ATO equipment over twenty years old, it was decided that this should not be replaced, and from 20th October 1986 the trains became one-person operated, with conventional driving operation, after train radio had been fitted.

The present 1960 tube stock passenger fleet comprises three three-car units (M-T-M) of which just two are required for service on the Hainault-Woodford branch of the Central Line on Mondays to Fridays, and one on Saturdays (a crew-operated four-car unit of 1962 stock has been used on Sundays since October 1987).

Trailer 4927 of 1938 stock, converted for use with 1960 stock DMs, resplendent in its original livery and seen at North Weald on 27th May 1990. R.J. Greenaway

A northbound Victoria Line train of 1967 Tube Stock arrives at King's Cross, with DM 3077 leading.
Capital Transport

Resulting from the successful trials with adapted 1960 tube stock for Automatic Train Operation on the 3.8-mile Central Line branch between Hainault and Woodford it was decided that the Victoria Line should be operated with automatic trains from its opening.

The stock for the Victoria Line was built by Metro-Cammell and was formed into four-car units (M-T-T-M), two such units being required for each train. The double-width car windows and 'pull-down' ventilators are features carried on from the 1960 stock motor cars. The passenger door windows are extended upwards to improve the vision for standing passengers, an idea tried out on 1938 stock car 10306 in 1949. For the train operator, maximum vision has been achieved by the provision of curved-round cab windows.

As on 1960 stock, the draught screens are set back from the door openings and the interior seating on DM cars is for 40 passengers. Trailer cars have longitudinal seats in the centre bay instead of transverse ones, providing a greater standing area, but the seating capacity is reduced in consequence to 36. Powerful headlights are fitted on the driving motor cars, one each side of the front cab door, and in addition to the twin red tail lights a stabling light is fitted. Illuminated advertisement panels are provided in all cars.

A combined 'traction/brake controller' is provided in the cab and takes the place of separate devices for motoring and braking. All motoring and braking positions required are therefore included on the one handle. A hydraulic handbrake, which is capable of holding a loaded train on the steepest gradient, is provided in each cab. Because of additional equipment provided on this stock (for ATO and for rheostatic braking) the motor alternator is located on the trailer cars.

Other innovations include a public address system, a 'carrier wave' communication system whereby the train operator can speak directly to the train regulator in the Cobourg Street (Euston) control room, a yellow 'calling on' light that can be illuminated to call a following train on for assistance, and communication between cabs on the train enabling the operator to speak to station staff at the rear of the train if the need arises.

The original order for 1967 stock was for 122 driving motor cars (61 'A' end north cars 3001–3061 and 61 'D' end south cars 3101–3161) and 122 trailers (4001–4061 and 4101–4161) to operate between Walthamstow and Victoria. When the extension south from Victoria to Brixton was authorised an additional 36 motor cars (3062–3079 and 3162–3179) and 36 trailers (4062–4079 and 4162–4179) were ordered, identical to the first batch except for trailer 4079 which has its body panels welded instead of riveted.

After being delivered to Ruislip depot and following commissioning, most units of 1967 stock were transferred to Hainault depot for ATO trials between Hainault and Woodford in four-car formations. After this, they were transferred to the Victoria Line depot at Northumberland Park. The first train of 1967 stock to arrive at Northumberland Park was that of units 3009 and 3011 on 1st April 1968. Enough trains had reached Northumberland Park to operate the first stage of the line, which was opened on 1st September 1968 between Walthamstow Central and Highbury & Islington.

All trains of 1967 stock can now be found on the Victoria Line, the practice of retaining one unit on the Central Line Hainualt-Woodford shuttle service ceasing in May 1984. The first unit to be overhauled at Northumberland Park depot instead of Acton Works was completed in July 1986 (unit 3021), all overhauls of 1967 stock now being done there.

Interior of 1967 stock in unmodified condition. The 1967 stock fleet is to be refurbished in similar style to the 1972 stock refurbishment illustrated on page 24, but with a Victoria Line colour scheme. LUL

The dramatic increase in passenger traffic required London Underground to consider additional trains for the Victoria Line. Plans were formulated to create an extra seven four-car units, by converting some units of 1972 MkI stock from the Northern Line. This was done at Acton Works between 1987 and 1989. The additional units are single-ended, the 1972 cars being formed in the middle of eight-car trains. The work not only involved renumbering of the 1972 converted cars, but also some of the 1967 stock cars involved with the scheme which gave 32 'A' end, 32 'D' end and 22 double-ended four-car units, making a line total of 43 eight-car trains, 3½ more than hitherto.

During 1989 and into early 1990, all Victoria Line trains were modified at Acton Works by having 'passenger alarm' fitted, along with improved public address and safety features. Two completed units (3010 and 3061) were selected for refurbishment work, this being done by Vic Berry of Leicester and Aston Martin-Tickford. The interiors were completely gutted and new lighting, flooring, panelling, seating and grab rails were fitted. The exteriors were painted in a livery of blue uppers, off-white with red cab ends and grey roofs. The train re-entered service on 9th October 1989. It has subsequently been decided that the whole Victoria Line fleet of 43 trains is to be refurbished by Vic Berry of Leicester and Aston Martin-Tickford, the first train (units 3005 and 3185) being despatched in June 1990. The exteriors are to be painted in what has since been decided to be the new livery — off-white with a blue 'skirt', red passenger doors and cab fronts, and grey roof.

An unpainted 1972 MkI stock train arrives at Chalk Farm on the southbound Northern Line. The leading DM carries the Stonebridge Park 'SP' depot overhaul logo. This station is still very much in original condition, as confirmed by the Yerkes tilework rings and the station name. Capital Transport

The Northern Line's 1972 MkI stock is very similar in appearance to the 1967 stock on the Victoria Line, but was built for crew operation. The stock is formed into three- and four-car units, one of each being required for each train (M-T-T-M+UNDM-T-M). The shunting control equipment for the uncoupling non-driving motor cars was obtained from withdrawn 1938 and 1949 tube stock UNDMs.

The total order comprised 90 driving motor cars, 90 trailers and 30 uncoupling non-driving motor cars, all in unpainted aluminium. The stock is numbered 3201—3230 ('A' end DMs), 3301—3330 ('D' end DMs), 3501—3530 ('D' end DMs with mechanical couplers only), 4201—4230, 4301—4330 and 4501—4530 (trailers) and 3401—3430 (UNDMs). External door-indicator lights were fitted, now a standard item on new stock. The first train entered service on the Northern on 26th June 1972 (units 3202 and 3502).

A further order for 1972 stock was later placed with Metro-Cammell for an additional 33 trains (known as 1972 MkII stock) and comprised 99 driving motor cars, 99 trailers and 33 uncoupling non-driving motor cars. The MkII stock is numbered 3231—3263 ('A' end DMs), 3331—3363 ('D' end DMs), 3531—3563 ('D' end DMs with mechanical couplers only), 4231—4263, 4331—4363 and 4531—4563 (trailers) and 3431—3463 (UNDMs). This second batch provided the rolling stock for stage one of the Jubilee Line which was opened to the public from 1st May 1979. Prior to that it was used on the Northern Line, allowing further 1938 stock trains to be withdrawn. The first trains of 1972 MkII stock entered service on 19th November 1973.

Although similar in appearance to the MkI cars, red-painted passenger doors were introduced on the MkII stock, and red roundels replaced 'Underground' transfers on the motor car sides as well as being introduced on the other cars. On MkII stock the set number is located in the offside cab window in the form of number plates.

When new, the seating moquette of the 1972 MkI stock was red/black/grey with red plastic armrests, while on the MkII this was green/blue with blue armrests.

Above **The 1972 MkII stock differs from the MkI in that it has red-painted passenger doors. At Queen's Park, the Bakerloo Line trains use the two inner platforms.** R.A. Ashman

DM 3304 of 1972 MkI stock painted in what was once intended to be LUL's Corporate livery, after return from painting by Vic Berry of Leicester. R.J. Greenaway

The trial refurbishment of UNDM 3429 involved half of the car being given a Northern Line decor and the other half, as shown here, a Bakerloo colour scheme. R.J. Greenaway

The chosen livery for LUL painted passenger stock is the 'red doors' livery with a blue skirt and white body as seen on DM 3302 at Morden. Capital Transport

Following the service reductions of December 1982, three fewer trains were required for the Jubilee Line (five since the line first opened in May 1979). Four MkII trains returned to the Northern Line during 1983 and were modified so that they were compatible with the MkI type. The first train with a combination of the two types ran on the Northern Line on 12th September 1983 (units 3210 and 3533).

With the entry into service of the 1983 stock on the Jubilee Line, a further 14 trains of 1972 MkII stock made their way to the Northern Line between November 1984 and November 1985. This allowed the 1938 stock to be withdrawn from the Bakerloo Line, by transferring more trains of 1959 stock from Northern Line.

In June 1985 unit 3203-4203-4303-3303 was withdrawn from service, providing the spares necessary for overhauling the 1972 stock fleet at Golders Green depot, which started in September 1985. This included the Jubilee Line's allocation of 1972 MkII stock, which necessitated transfer between Neasden and Golders Green, completed in early 1987. Following this, Stonebridge Park depot commenced overhauls of the Northern Line's 1972 MkI stock. Unit 3203-4203-4303-3303 is now being prepared for return to service.

The delivery of the 1983 (batch II) stock for the Jubilee Line allowed the 1972 MkII stock on that line to be transferred to the Bakerloo, which was achieved in March 1989. While on the Bakerloo Line, the 1972 MkII stock operates 'wrong way round', in that the 'D' ends face north and the 'A' ends face south. This is to allow shunting operations in Stonebridge Park depot to be carried out from a middle (33xx) motor car rather than from an UNDM car. OPO on the Bakerloo Line commenced on 20th November 1989.

To create 3½ additional trains to increase Victoria Line services, five four-car and four three-car units of 1972 MkI stock were converted at Acton Works during 1987-89. Four UNDM cars subsequently became redundant. Two are currently in store, while the other two have been used for trials in the refurbishment programme.

Three trains of 1972 MkI stock on the Northern Line were painted in various trial liveries during 1989. Units 3204 and 3522 are finished in the same style as the Victoria Line train described in the previous chapter, while 3227 and 3518 were painted in 'blue doors' livery (off-white all over, including roof, red cab ends and blue doors). The last train to be painted (3202 and 3523) is in the livery since decided to become standard — off white with blue 'skirt', red doors and grey roof (known as the 'red doors' livery).

During 1989 and 1990, all 1972 MkI stock on the Northern Line was modified with the 'passenger alarm' system. For the future, both batches of 1972 stock are to be refurbished and painted in the new livery, units 3249, 3256, 3543 and 3558 being the first.

An eastbound Piccadilly Line train of 1973 Tube Stock arrives at Arnos Grove. When new, a few units had black roofs with the majority being finished in white. Overhauled units now have their roofs painted grey. R.J. Waterhouse

In order to provide new stock for the Piccadilly Line, orders were placed with Metro-Cammell for $87\frac{1}{2}$ six-car trains, comprising 196 driving motor cars, 175 trailers and 154 uncoupling non-driving motor cars. Each car is about six feet longer than cars of earlier stock but the total length of a six-car train is about 17 feet shorter than a seven-car 1956/59 stock train. This enables the complete train to fit into the platforms at all tube stations on the line, necessary as the stock was subsequently converted to one-person operation. The first train entered service on 19th July 1975 as a passenger-carrying special when the extension from Hounslow West to Hatton Cross was opened, formed of units 108 and 137. The first normal passenger working occurred on 18th August 1975, comprising units 140 and 141.

The majority of trains are formed M-T-UNDM+UNDM-T-M. The driving motor cars at each end are provided with mechanical couplers only, the UNDM cars being fitted with automatic couplers. In addition there are 21 three-car units formed M-T-M known as 'double-cab' units, with automatic couplers on each driving motor car. The purpose of these units is to enable the replacement of a three-car unit fitted with an UNDM when required for maintenance, without making the other three cars unavailable for service. The 1973 stock is numbered 100—253 (DMs), 854—895 (DMs with automatic couplers for double-cab units), 300—453 (UNDMs), 500—653 (trailers) and even numbers only from 654—694 (trailers used in double-cab units).

Improvements incorporated in this stock are the provision of an air-operated cab door, being operated independently from the passenger doors, a 'selective close' button for the passenger doors, enabling in bad weather all except one single and one single leaf of a double door on each car to remain closed at terminal stations, the Westcode electro-pneumatic braking system, enabling the Westinghouse air brake to be omitted, a train equipment fault-finding panel for the driver's use, automatic wheel slip/slide protection, and load control of acceleration and braking. The motor alternator (located on the trailer cars of 1967 and 1972 stocks) is fitted on the driving motors (as on 1962 stock and before) and UNDMs.

Unlike the 1967 and 1972 stock trailer cars, interior seating in all 1973 stock cars is arranged longitudinally at each end with transverse seats in the centre bay, each car seating 44 passengers. The ventilators above the double-glazed car windows are of a sliding type and not the pull-down type as on 1960, 1967 and 1972 stocks. The train number panel incorporates numbers of the 'flapper' type, instead of metal or (on newer stock) plastic plates. At the driving end of each driving motor car a deep red band is painted below the cab windows. It was originally proposed to fit ceiling-mounted extractor fans (three per car) to all 1973 stock cars when new, but owing to design difficulties the first sets were not fitted until October 1977, on cars 130-530-330+427-627-227. Most trains now have fans fitted.

Small detail differences exist between the earlier and later cars of 1973 stock. The first 16 units (100—115) have black roofs, the later ones being white. The first 18 units (100—117) and units 178, 179, 202 and 203 have higher waist-level panelling joints than the rest. Twenty-five west-end single-cab unit trailers have been fitted with de-icing equipment.

Because of delays in commissioning, several units of 1973 stock were stored at the Bicester Military Railway and at the Metro-Cammell factory prior to or after delivery to London Transport. Some of the stored units from Bicester were delivered the wrong way round (the 'A' end facing east and 'D' end facing west) and had to be turned before entering service on the Piccadilly Line.

On Friday 16th December 1977, Her Majesty the Queen opened the Piccadilly Line extension from Hatton Cross to Heathrow Central. The train on which the Queen travelled during the ceremony comprised cars 244-644-444+445-645-245 and carried a special headboard.

DM 208 was damaged in a collision at Northfields in May 1978, and during repair it was fitted with prototype 1983 tube stock bogies designed by Gloucester with a Metro-Cammell built body bolster. So that the experimental bogies could be tested as a three-car train, single-cab DM 208 took the place of double-cab DM 888 in March 1979, making two reformed units. The units reverted to normal in October 1981.

The last two double-cab units of 1973 stock were delivered with experimental Thyristor 'Chopper' control, one with Westinghouse equipment (892-692-893) and the other with GEC equipment (894-694-895). The two units were dubbed the Experimental Tube Train (ETT) and the Westinghouse unit was delivered in two portions at the end of 1977, being transferred to Northfields on 17th March 1978 for test running between Acton Town and Northfields, for which 1938 stock three-car unit 10306-012498-11247 was utilised as a pilot unit until the end of January 1979, when it was withdrawn. The ETT was transferred to Hainault on 27th February 1979 for further testing, between Roding Valley and Grange Hill on the Hainault and Woodford loop in non-traffic hours. Daytime test running of the train between Hainault and Woodford commenced in November 1982 and it entered passenger service from 25th July 1983. The GEC-equipped ETT was delivered on 18th September 1979 and was prepared for test running during 1980, being transferred to Northfields on 17th September. When tests were concluded it was decided to convert both units to standard, to provide one extra full-length train for the Piccadilly Line. The GEC ETT entered Acton Works for conversion car-by-car in early-1984, being completed and returned to Northfields depot on 16th August 1985. It is fitted with Davies and Metcalfe braking equipment and entered passenger service for the first time as a conventional unit on 12th February 1986. Westinghouse ETT 892-692-893 was transferred from Hainault to Acton Works on 23rd June 1985 for conversion to standard. This was completed in October 1986 and the unit entered service on the Piccadilly Line on 10th April 1987.

On 1st April 1986 Their Royal Highnesses the Prince and Princess of Wales officially opened the new Terminal 4 station and buildings at Heathrow Airport, for which 1973 stock units 864 and 195 were used, being given a special headboard and side 'Concorde' stickers, as well as a special 'Terminal 4' destination blind. Passenger services commenced on 12th April, but Piccadilly Line trains worked non-stop through the new station and around the new single-track loop from the new timetable on 7th April. One-way loop workings cause trains to becomed 'turned' and unless an even number of trips is worked, which is impossible to guarantee with the operating complexities of the Piccadilly Line, some trains finish at the end of the day the opposite way round. As the 1973 stock is unable to couple 'A' to 'A' and 'D' to 'D' for operational purposes, the two ex-ETT units give additional stock to assist in overcoming the problem of trains stabled the wrong way round.

When new, unit 114-514-314 was used (along with 315-515-115) to train crews on the new stock at Cockfosters. When this was completed, unit 114 was used to provide spare parts for other cars of 1973 stock. Trailer 514 was used in 1982 for ventilation experiments prior to the arrival of the 1983 stock. It returned to Metro-Cammell in December 1981 for this experimental equipment to be fitted, returning to Ruislip depot on 18th February 1982 by road. It was tested on the Piccadilly and Jubilee Lines until April 1982 in the formation 152-514-352. The car was converted back to standard by the end of 1982, once again becoming spare with UNDM 314. On 11th August 1982, double-ended DM 888 was badly damaged by fire in an incident between Wood Green and Bounds Green, its place being taken in January 1983 by DM 114. The revised formation of 114-688-889 entered service on 31st March 1983, this being the first occasion for DM 114.

Trailer 514 left Northfields depot by road for BREL at Derby on 19th December 1985 for conversion to a purpose-built track recording car, completion of which was made in 1987. It is numbered TRC666 and works between converted 1960 stock DMs 3901 and 3905, which have been renumbered L132 and L133. UNDM 314 continues to be stored in unserviceable condition at Northfields depot, having served in 1984/5 as a temporary canteen, along with DM 888.

With the transfer of overhauling stock from Acton Works to depots, Cockfosters took on the role for the 1973 stock, the first unit of which (315-515-115) was completed in June 1986.

The first of the deep-level tube lines to be converted to one-person operation was the Piccadilly Line, operative from 31st August 1987. The 1973 stock was converted for OPO at Northfields depot (all single-ended units and two double-cab units) and Acton Works (the remaining double-cab units) during 1986 and up to September 1987. The exterior differences include the fitting of an offside window wiper and calling-on light. (When the stock was new, a calling-on light was fitted on the driver's side of the destination blind, but was later replaced by an opening for cab ventilation). In the operator's cab, door control buttons have been provided on the console and a new operator's seat fitted. From 31st August 1987, the date of OPO introduction on the Piccadilly Line, the operation of the passenger emergency alarm system was changed so that drivers could take the train on to the next station in the event of a passenger using the alarm.

Interior view of 1973 stock. Brian Hardy

DM 3637 of 1983 (Batch II) stock at the rear of a Jubilee Line train at Wembley Park. John Laker

The 1983 stock has a number of features that were new to tube stock, some of which had already been incorporated successfully in the D stock. The front of the train has flat but deeper driving cab windows, incorporating shatterproof glass to give greater protection to the driver. Single-leaf doors supersede double doors on all cars, and the opening of these is by push-buttons operated by passengers. The layout provides space for four extra seats per car, increasing the seating capacity in each to 48. The seats are covered in similar moquette to that used on D stock (yellow/orange/brown/black). Yellow melamine panelling is fitted inside, except at passenger door positions, where orange is used.

Seven of the earlier units to be delivered (3601–6/8) were returned to Metro-Cammell between October and December 1984 for bodywork modifications to be made. This included altering the all-round stainless steel grab rail by the passenger doors (which was continuous from floor level across the ceiling and down to the floor on the other side) to be from floor to ceiling only with a separate grab rail over the doors. These seven units arrived back at Neasden between January and March 1985. The remainder of the fleet (units 3607/9–30) were delivered with these modifications incorporated. A further change during construction was a reduction in the number of ventilation openings over the destination blind, which became standard from unit 3613. Units 3601–6/8 also had this modification carried out when returned to Metro-Cammell for body strengthening and thus units 3607/9–12 are the only ones remaining with the original closely-spaced vents.

The first train to carry passengers (units 3607 and 3609) did so on a press demonstration on 2nd May 1984, but normal passenger operation commenced from 8th May 1984.

In late-1986 authority was given for further trains of 1983 stock, in order to restore rolling stock and services near to pre-December 1982 levels. This new order comprised 16½ six-car trains and was numbered as follows: 'A' DMs 3631–3663, 'D' DMs 3731–3763 and trailers 4631–4663, of which 4631–4635 have de-icing equipment. Although almost identical to the first batch of stock, the 1983 (batch II) differs in that the red/blue Underground bullseye replaces the solid red roundel, car numbers are in blue, and interior car lighting is with standard fluorescent tubes, as on 1967/72/73 stocks, and not with luminators as on batch I. The first unit of the new order (3636–4636–3736) was received at Neasden depot on 11th October 1987 and entered service on 27th November 1987.

The only active train of 1986 Tube Stock is the 'blue train' built by BREL. Two such cars are seen on the test tracks between South Ealing and Acton Town. David Rowe

The replacement rolling stock for the Central Line, construction of which is now in progress, is the result of extensive trials conducted with three four-car prototype trains known as the 1986 Prototype Tube Stock. These three prototypes tested new materials and construction methods, and experimented with different interior seating layouts.

Two of the four-car prototypes were built by Metro-Cammell of Birmingham and the third by BREL Ltd of Derby. Electrical equipment for one of the Metro-Cammell trains was provided by GEC Traction of Manchester, and for the other by Brown-Boveri of Zurich, Switzerland. Brush Electrical Machines of Loughborough provided the equipment for the BREL train. Each of the three trains was finished in a distinctive colour. To give a feeling of spaciousness, the two Metro-Cammell trains had windows in the car ends and on all trains the side windows extend up into the curve of the roof.

Each of the prototypes consisted of two two-car units, one car having a driving cab and the other no cab. The automatic coupling arrangements between units and the controls of all three trains were designed to be compatible so that any combination of two-car units could couple to form a four-car, six-car or an eight-car train. The car bodies and the floor structure were constructed from wide aluminium extrusions welded together, which make them both lighter and cheaper to manufacture than existing tube car bodies. This form of construction requires external sliding doors which do not need 'pockets' in the body structure.

The three trains were formed and numbered thus:

Formation:	DM	— NDM	+ NDM	— DM
Train 'A'	11	21	22	12
Train 'B'	13	23	24	14
Train 'C'	15	25	26	16

Train 'C' was the first to be delivered on 25th October 1986, followed by BREL train 'B' on 15th November 1986. Train 'A' was the last to arrive on 21st March 1987. Following extensive testing, the trains operated spasmodically in passenger service between 4th May 1988 and 14th August 1989 in six-car formations on the Jubilee Line. The BREL four-car train is now based at Northfields for test train work, while the two Metro-Cammell trains are stored at Neasden depot.

An order for 85 trains of Central Line Replacement Stock was placed in 1989 with BREL, Derby. Each train will comprise eight cars formed of four two-car units. There will be three combinations of two-car unit and three types of individual vehicle. Car 'A' will be a driving motor car with cab, shoes, traction equipment and automatic coupler. Car 'B' will be a non-driving motor car, having no cab or shoes, but will have traction equipment which will be fed from the adjacent motor car. It will also have a shunting control cabinet at its outer end along with an automatic coupler. Car type 'C' will similarly be a non-driving motor car having no cab, but will have shoes and traction equipment as an 'A' car, a shunting control cabinet and automatic coupler at its outer end.

With these three types of car, semi-permanent two-car units will be formed as follows: 175 A-B units; 133 B-C units; 32 B-C de-icing units. All the two-car units will be fully reversible and compatible and thus there will be no distinction between 'A' and 'D' ends as hitherto. Car numbering will be as follows:

Car type A 91001-91349 odd numbers	Total 175 cars
Car type B 92001-92349 odd numbers in A-B units	} Total 340 cars
Car type B 92002-92266 even numbers in B-C units	
Car type B 92402-92464 even numbers in B-C de-icing units	
Car type C 93002-93266 even numbers in B-C units	} Total 165 cars
Car type C 93402-93464 even numbers in B-C de-icing units	

With the different combination of cars and units, it will be possible for an eight-car train to be formed in one of 36 different ways.

Each car will have all longitudinal seating arranged six per side in the outer bays and five per side in the centre saloon bay (i.e. between the double doors), giving a total of 34 seats per car. The middle pair of each group of six will be set back six inches to allow greater standing capacity, at which point there will also be a floor-to-ceiling grab pole in the centre. At non-cabbed ends (at the trailing end of car 'A', and both ends of cars 'B' and 'C') there will be one perch seat in each corner position. The interior colour scheme will be in soft stone with seating moquette in warm red/ivory/blue arranged in diagonally split squares. Car floors will be of a rubber type material in grey/blue terrazzo chip. Grab rails will be of the all-round type as on 1986 prototype train 'A', but at the set-back seat positions the handrails will go up into the car roof. The large single-glazed car windows, which curve up into the roof line, have been adopted from prototype train 'C'.

Passenger door control buttons will be provided. Open buttons will be in the middle of the door separations inside and out, while extra open buttons will be fitted inside to the 'stand-back' pillars, one each side, along with door close buttons. The passenger door width will be 1664mm (double) and 832mm (single), each leaf being some 6 inches wider than on the prototype trains to allow speedier alighting and boarding and thereby reducing station stop times. Like the prototype trains, sliding doors will be externally hung. Apart from the driving end of the 'A' cars, end windows will be provided to give greater passenger security. Other interior features will include illuminated route line diagrams (mimic diagrams) and pre-programmed announcements in digitised speech. The exteriors will be painted in the new corporate livery — off-white, grey roof, blue skirt, red doors and cab front.

The driver's cab will incorporate in-cab closed circuit television, provided by Siemens/BREL. In addition to public address, in the event of an emergency, there will be two-way communication between the driver and passengers. The driver will have a redesigned fore/aft traction brake controller, which will be positioned on the right-hand side of the driver's seat — reminiscent of that provided on the 1935 streamlined tube stock!

The thyristor controlled traction equipment is being provided by a consortium of Assea Brown Boveri of Switzerland and Brush Electrical Machines of Loughborough. A computer data transmission system with multiplexing will be used for much of the electrical control of the trains. This reduces the number of cables but safety circuits such as braking, are separately wired as well. The Westinghouse analogue braking system will be fitted, along with air suspension. The bogies will be provided by Kawasaki Heavy Industries of Osaka, Japan. Each car will have six BREL Stone International ventilation units giving full forced ventilation.

The length of each car will be 16248mm over body ends, 2620mm wide over door leaves and 2869mm high at the top of the car roof. Construction of the new Central Line trains started in the late summer of 1990 and the first train to be delivered is anticipated for September 1991 with entry into service scheduled for March 1992. The completion of delivery for the 85 trains is currently expected in late-1994.

A mock-up of the
proposed 1990 stock
for the Central Line in
the London
Transport Museum
on display in the
'Tube Centenary'
exhibition.
R.J. Greenaway

DM 5093 of A60 stock approaches Hillingdon on the Uxbridge branch of the Metropolitan Line. Along with trains on the Amersham line, most Uxbridge trains now operate to and from the City (Aldgate or Moorgate) daily. This unit was the first to be overhauled at Neasden in July 1987 and, along with six others, has maroon painted car roofs. R.J. Waterhouse

To coincide with the electrification of the Metropolitan Line from Rickmansworth to Amersham and Chesham and the provision of two additional tracks from Harrow-on-the-Hill to north of Moor Park (Watford South Junction, where the Watford line diverges), new cars to be known as A60 stock were ordered from Cravens Ltd. The stock comprised 124 driving motor cars and 124 trailers, being formed into four-car units (M-T-T-M). Numbering is 5000–5123 (DMs) and 6000–6123 (trailers). The first train of A60 stock entered passenger service on 12th June 1961 (units 5004 and 5008).

A further order of A stock, almost identical to the first batch, was provided to replace the F and P stocks on the Uxbridge line. This second batch was designated A62 stock and comprised 108 driving motor cars (5124–5231) and 108 trailers (6124–6231). The A62 stock followed on without interruption after the A60 batch and all A stock trains were in service by December 1963. All driving motor cars were provided with automatic couplers, similar to those introduced on the 1960 tube stock, enabling any driving motor car to be coupled to another.

Interior seating was arranged transversely with an off-centre gangway allowing two-passenger seats on one side and three-passenger seats on the other. The DM cars seat 54 and have in addition four tip-up seats at the end furthest from the cab. Small luggage racks are provided above the windows.

A60 and A62 stock units were interchangeable until converted for OPO, and operated in eight-car formations of two four-car units. The practice of operating single four-car units in off-peak times was discontinued in 1981. However, the Chalfont-Chesham shuttle service is operated by a single unit and four-car trains have operated on the Metropolitan East London branch from June 1977 until the end of April 1985 and from 9th May 1987.

In 1974 tinted glass was experimentally fitted in the windows of trailer car 6096. A62 stock DM car 5208 and trailer 6208 have been fitted with thermostatically-controlled car heaters. A62 stock DM car 5218 was equipped with air-metacone suspension in 1966, which proved sufficiently successful to be incorporated in the C69 stock. This form of suspension enables the car height to be maintained at the same level irrespective of the load, and by measuring the load of individual cars in a complete train is used to provide differential acceleration and braking. Car 5218 was fitted in 1976 with prototype D stock bogies incorporating a new suspension in the form of air bags at Metro-Cammell works, Birmingham, and also a spring-applied parking brake. The air bags system was designed by the Gloucester Railway Carriage & Wagon Company.

One of the A stock units in 'blue doors' livery is seen at Chesham, well away from its normal haunt of the East London Line.
R.J. Waterhouse

DM 5056 has the livery with blue upper half, the second unadopted scheme. Repainting of the East London Line units was financially supported by the London Docklands Development Corporation.
David Rowe

Changes to unit formations have been rare, compared with some other stocks, and can be summarised thus: DM car 5171 replaced 5091 in April 1977 until the latter's repair was completed at Acton Works in mid-1978, DM 5171 having been spare (with 6171) since a previous mishap in August 1975 which resulted in sister cars 5170 and 6170 eventually being scrapped at Neasden in June 1981. In April 1981 DM 5043 replaced 5056, giving the formation 5043-6056-6057-5057, the first (and only) time that a 'D' end DM has been used in an 'A' position, demonstrating the versatility of the A stock. This reverted to normal in October 1982, after the repair of DMs 5042 and 5056.

Two mishaps in the summer of 1981 and another two in 1983 led to two more hybrid formations: 5008-6034-6035-5035 and 5138-6092-6093-5093 respectively, with the latter returning to normal in April 1986. A more serious collision occurred at Kilburn in December 1984, after which the following cars were salvaged and later returned to service: 5028-6028-6117-5117. Plans were formulated to convert and adapt the A60/62 stock for eventual

The livery style decided on in summer 1990 for the programme of refurbishments.
F.W. Ivey

Interior of refurbished A62 stock DM 5133, the appearance of which has been greatly changed. Gone are the ceiling-high draught screens and the ceiling bulkheads have been re-profiled.
Brian Hardy

one-person operation, which would require major alterations but which would be much cheaper than opting for new stock and scrapping trains that were only about halfway through their life. Fifty-six of the original 58 eight-car trains have been converted for OPO, some at Ruislip, but mostly at Acton Works, although it was the original intention for it to be the other way round. To economise in the number of cabs requiring conversion, the stock was divided into 44 'A' end units, 44 'D' end units and 24 double-ended units.

Car 5008 was renumbered 5034 in July 1985 while 5028-6028-6117-5117 were renumbered at the end of the A stock series to 5232-6232-6233-5233 at about the same time. The designation of particular 'ends' from OPO conversion has meant that the once versatile A stock has lost its previous operating flexibility, with only 'A' and 'D' ends being able to be coupled. In addition, only OPO-converted cabs have train radio fitted. The first converted train in crew-operating mode to be operated was formed of units 5038 and 5227 on 19th November 1985.

OPO conversion started in April 1985 and visible alterations include the fitting of public address, two new pneumatic windscreen wipers, powerful twin headlights, a slightly smaller depth driver's window with missile-proof glass, and door controls in the cabs. These modifications apply only to operative cabs. All DMs, however, have 'A' and 'D' stickers at their respective ends and guards panels have been removed at the trailing ends of the passenger saloon.

In 1987 three more cars of withdrawn A stock were scrapped (5029, 5116 and 5171), leaving four DMs (5008 — the original 5034, 5009, 5036 and 5037) and six trailers (6008, 6009, 6029, 6037, 6116 and 6171) awaiting disposal. In 1986 trailer 6036 was converted at Acton Works into a 'Rail Treatment Car', to dispense Sandite (an adhesion improver) on running rails. This is particularly necessary north of Rickmansworth on the Metropolitan Line each autumn, in the leaf-fall season. The converted car was formed into a four-car double-ended unit of A stock (making five cars in all) and underwent tests in the autumn of 1986. Tests were successful and in 1987 the train again worked during the leaf-fall season, formed 5120-6036-6120-6121-5209. During its period of non-use after the 1986 experiments, the body of car 6036 was repainted off-white and its roof in Metropolitan Line maroon, and trial blue lettering/car numbers were applied, prior to adopting a policy for future A stock overhauls at Neasden, which started in mid-1987. Other experiments tried prior to this included painting the domes of DMs 5139 (middle) and 5193 (leading 'D' end) dark blue, as an alternative roof colour, but both of these cars now have standard grey roof domes. Resulting from all this, the first unit of A stock overhauled at Neasden (5092) was outshopped in July 1987, sporting a maroon roof, car numbers in blue with red lining, and red/blue Underground roundels. A total of seven units (5092, 5052, 5002, 5020, 5048, 5042 and 5050) were given maroon roofs, and three others (5074, 5068 and 5044) red roofs. Other experiments since overhauls started include 'METROPOLITAN' replacing the roundels on cars 5020 and 5021 (only one 'METROPOLITAN' currently survives), and a black painted section under the driver's window of 5048 (and most subsequently overhauled units), to give a more 'balanced' front end appearance. On overhauls from June 1988, roof colours have reverted to being grey. Inside the cars, nine units were fully painted in having red-painted doors and melamine and two-tone grey panels.

The seven units of A stock that work the East London Line have been exterior painted. Unit 5066 was completed first at Ruislip in November 1988 in off-white with blue doors, grey roof and red cab ends. The other six units followed in 1989-90 but these were painted by Vic Berry of Leicester where they were taken by road from and to Ruislip (initially) and (later) Neasden. Units 5058, 5062, 5064 and 5232 were painted similarly to 5066 (with minor differences), while unit 5056 was painted in off-white below waist level and blue above waist level, but still with red cab ends and grey roof. The last unit to be painted (5122) is in 'red doors' livery — off-white with blue 'skirt', red doors and cab ends and a white roof. This is the livery that is to be used on all future painting schemes for passenger stock, except that the roof colour is to be grey. As the A stock for the East London Line is maintained at Neasden, it is not uncommon for these painted units to work occasionally on the Metropolitan Line to Uxbridge, Watford and Amersham.

In preparation for future refurbishment of A stock, two cars (5132 and 6132) were selected for trials. The work was done by Metro-Cammell in 1989 and the exteriors were painted as with unit 5056. Inside trailer 6132, panelling and seating moquette was replaced and new flooring fitted. More substantial changes were made to the inside of 5132 and both cars were given pull-back hopper windows. It was decided, however, that further trials were required and the complete four-car unit (5132-6132-6133-5133) returned to Metro-Cammell in February 1990. The four-car unit was delivered back to Neasden in early June 1990 and the exterior has been painted into 'red doors' livery with grey roof. Inside, the colour scheme is cream and pale pink with a dark grey area around ankle level. Floor-to-ceiling grab poles have been fitted and these, along with other grab poles, are finished in pale blue. The old draught screens to the ceilings have been replaced by those finishing at head height only. New vandal-resistant car seats are individually shaped and a new moquette has been used. All four cars have hopper windows in place of the former tilting quarter lights. The unit re-entered service on 8th August 1990 and it is anticipated that the refurbishing of the rest of the A stock fleet will commence in 1991. In addition, eight cars that have been out of service at Neasden depot for between six and 15 years, are to be refurbished and returned to service. The eight cars, 5008 (formerly 5034), 6008, 6009, 5009, 5036, 6037, 6116 and 5037, were taken by road from Neasden to BREL Derby in August 1990, and will form two additional double-ended de-icing units.

Diverted off its normal District Line route to Wimbledon, a C stock train with DM 5544 nearest the camera is seen at Ealing Broadway, about to return to High Street Kensington. C69 and C77 types are operationally fully compatible, although some eight years separate their build. David Rowe

The Circle and Hammersmith & City Lines were operated by six-car trains of converted CO and CP stock until the delivery of the C69 stock enabled the CO/CP stock to be transferred to the District Line to replace the last of the Q stock. The first train of C69 stock entered service on 28th September 1970 (units 5522, 5523 and 5524) and all were in service by December 1971.

The new stock comprised 106 driving motor cars (5501—5606) and 106 trailers (6501—6606), formed into two-car semi-permanently coupled units (M-T). All units were identical and at the outer ends of each a fully-automatic reversible coupler was fitted. The six cars for each train could therefore be formed M-T+T-M+T-M or M-T+M-T +T-M.

Each car has four sets of double passenger doors on each side, with seating capacity reduced in consequence to 32. On the lines on which the stock operates, the majority of passenger journeys are of short distances and so the additional doors were introduced to allow increased speed in boarding and alighting in busy periods. Each pair of doors is separated by double-glazed car windows. On the driving motor cars the cab door is also air operated, being independently controlled. The door control panels are located in the cab, as on the O stock previously working on the Hammersmith & City Line. Public address is fitted to enable the driver to make announcements to the passengers. A 'selective close' facility is provided, whereby all but one pair of doors can be kept closed at terminal stations in cold weather.

Air-metacone suspension has been incorporated in the new cars, after successful trials on A62 stock car 5218. Rheostatic braking as on 1967 tube stock is also fitted. Provision was made in the design for the trains to be easily converted to one-man operation and all cars have since been adapted. Ceiling-mounted fans are located at each door position for heating and ventilation, which is thermostatically-controlled. A hydraulic parking brake is fitted in each DM cab, and all cars have illuminated interior advertisement panels.

The trailing ends of the saloons of the C stock refurbished unit have been fitted with windows to give greater passenger security, as seen on C69 trailer 6585 in Acton Works. R.J. Greenaway

Interior of refurbished C77 DM car 5585. The seating moquette underneath the car windows was removed before the train re-entered service. Capital Transport

Facing Page The latest mock-up of the interior of how the C stock will look like after refurbishment. This design has been proposed by Cre'active and the refurbishment work is being done by RFS Engineering of Doncaster. Cre'active

Motor car 5585 was damaged beyond repair in a bomb incident in March 1976 and was scrapped. An additional C77 motor car was built to replace it. Trailer car 6585, not so badly damaged, was repaired at Acton Works. Its black roof was altered to become unpainted with silver-painted domes to match the C77 cars. The first unit of C69 stock was overhauled at Acton Works in September 1978. DM 5524 had its black roof changed to unpainted, whereas trailer 6524 retained its black roof. Other C69 units overhauled have retained the black roofs, while the C77 units overhauled retained their white or unpainted roofs. Overhaul at Acton Works of C stock ceased in November 1985 and subsequent overhauls have been undertaken at Upminster (District Line) depot, the first unit, 5708, being completed in August 1986. Up to mid-1987, only C77 stock had been overhauled at Upminster, but following the completion of these units, a start was made on the outstanding C69 stock

(units 5588 to 5606), which were given a minor internal refurbishment in the late-1970s. It has since been decided that all future C69 stock black roofs will be repainted white on overhaul, the first to be completed being 5588-6588 in September 1987.

To replace the six-car trains of CO/CP stock operating the Wimbledon to Edgware Road section of the District Line, eleven six-car trains of C77 stock were ordered from Metro-Cammell. Delivery commenced in July 1977. The cars are similar to the C69 stock operating on the Hammersmith & City and Circle Lines, and likewise are formed into two-car reversible units (M-T) with an automatic coupler at each outer end. In consequence, the maintenance of C77 stock trains is carried out at Hammersmith (Metropolitan Line) depot. The first train of C77 stock entered service on the Hammersmith & City Line on 12th December 1977 (units 5701, 5702 and 5703).

A C77 stock unit enters Edgware Road on the District Line service from Wimbledon. David Rowe

Interior car heating on C69 stock is by means of ceiling-mounted heater blowers at the double-door positions. Cars of C77 stock were delivered with heater panels below the draught screen at floor level, covered with black aerowalk material. However, during 1979/80 additional heaters were fitted up to draught screen level, covered with blue aerowalk. All 33 units, including replacement car 5585, had been treated by October 1980.

After years of negotiation between management and unions, one-person operation with C stock was introduced on the Hammersmith & City Line from 26th March 1984. The Circle Line followed suit from 22nd October 1984 and the Wimbledon-Edgware Road section of the District Line (along with the District main line) from 4th November 1985.

The C stock then entered a period of relative stability until consideration was given to refurbishing it. C77/69 stock unit 5585-6585 was chosen as the prototype and work was undertaken at BREL, Derby in 1989. The exterior of both cars was painted in blue above waist level and white beneath, with a red driving cab front and grey roof. Both cars have had the maple wood flooring replaced by light grey grooved moulded flooring and the trailing ends have been fitted with windows to improve visibility between cars, thus enhancing passenger security. Other changes include the fitting of a spring-applied parking brake and the passenger emergency handles have been replaced by an alarm push button system. Inside DM 5585 new seating moquette and suspended rectangular yellow grab rails for standing passengers have been fitted. More substantial changes have been made to trailer 6585, where the transverse seats have all been replaced by longitudinal seating, with the loss of six seat positions. The fitting of a shunting control cabinet to the uncoupling end of 6585 has caused the loss of one further seat and thus the number of seats in this car is reduced from 32 to 25, although standing capacity has been greatly increased. The ceiling bulkheads in 6585 have been redesigned, eliminating the illuminated advertisement positions, while the draught screens have been reduced in size — the grab poles and glass now slant inwards towards the body above waist level.

Having been displayed to the public, the unit entered service on 22nd November 1989. It has since been decided that the whole C stock fleet is to be refurbished during 1990-92 and the first two trains (5726+5543+5569 and 5566+5582+5706) plus unit 5539 are currently at RFS Doncaster for the work to be done. Neither of the designs used in cars 5585 and 6585 have been adopted; instead a new interior design by design consultants Cre'active has been chosen.

D stock DM 7026 leads a six-car train into Victoria. Red and blue Underground roundels have now replaced the solid red roundels on this stock. The British Railways totem below the destination blind is a non-standard fitting! Capital Transport

The D stock comprises 75 trains which replaced the bulk of the District Line's CO/CP and R stocks between 1980 and 1983. Each train is composed of six cars, but each car is about 60ft long and a train of D stock is approximately the same length as the seven-car train it replaced. The train formation is as used for the 1973 tube stock on the Piccadilly Line. Most trains have two single-cab units with automatic couplers on the middle UNDM cars, and 65 east and 65 west facing single cab units have been built. Twenty double-cab units with automatic couplers at each driving end have also been built, and these units were the first type to be delivered. D stock is numbered 7000–7129 (DMs), 7500–7539 (DMs with automatic couplers), 8000–8129 (UNDMs), 17000–17129 (trailers) and even numbers only from 17500–17538 (trailers used in double-cab units).

Each of the four passenger doorways on each side of the car is 3ft 6ins wide, 1ft less than each double doorway on CO/CP and R stocks, and a single leaf sliding door is fitted at each opening. Draught screens are set back from the door openings by about 8ins. DM cars seat 44, trailers and UNDMs seat 48. One transverse seat bay on each side of the car is provided in the centre section of all cars; all other seats are longitudinal.

A modified form of passenger door control (PDC) is incorporated with illuminating 'Press to Open' buttons for passenger use. Each doorway has three 'passenger open' buttons, two inside and one outside. The 'selective close' facility for passenger comfort is provided as on C69/77 stock, and a new 'selective reopen' facility is installed whereby it is possible to reopen only the doors on those cars where they have failed to close properly. The door controls are located in the driving cabs.

To improve riding quality, a new type of bogie was tested on A62 stock car 5218 for use on D stock. This incorporates suspension using two hemispherical rubber cushions supporting a coil spring and replaces an earlier plan to use air bags. The motors and wheel sets are interchangeable with those on 1973 tube stock. Fans are installed in the car ceilings for ventilation and 'Pyro-bar' type car heaters are also installed.

A new type of driver's control handle is incorporated, operated in the 'fore' and 'aft' positions. This type of controller was tried out on the experimental 1935 tube stock, but the handle has to be kept twisted while the train is in motion (this position being equivalent to the dead man's handle) and moved forward for motoring and back for braking. The driver's seat is a swivelling design instead of 'pull down' and adjusts up and down as well as forwards and backwards. As on 1973 tube stock, a fault-finding Train Equipment Panel (TEP) is

A westbound District Line train of D stock enters Earl's Court on a working to Richmond.
R.J. Waterhouse

provided (with modifications) as are air-operated sliding cab doors. A spring-applied parking brake is fitted instead of the hydraulic type fitted to previous stocks. Only one compressor is fitted on each single-cab unit, but the double-cab units each have two.

The first unit of D stock was delivered on 29th June 1979 to Ruislip depot and was transferred to Ealing Common for commissioning on the same day. The commissioning of all D stock was undertaken at Ealing Common, being taken there from Ruislip between CO/CP and, later, R stock pilot units specially adapted for the purpose.

The first train of D stock entered passenger service on Monday 28th January 1980 and was formed of cars 7532-17532-7533+7528-17528-7529. The train developed a door defect during the morning peak and was substituted later that morning by one comprising cars 7516-17516-7517+7538-17538-7539. The first train of single-cab units (7000-17000-8000+8001-17001-7001) was delivered on 25th January 1980, and the first train of this type to enter service (7008-17008-8008+8009-17009-7009) did so on 21st April 1980. The first 25 trailers in west end single-cab units (17000/2/4 up to 17048) have been equipped with de-icing equipment.

Unit 8043-17043-7043, delivered in November 1980, is fitted with Knorr-Bremse experimental braking equipment, which is of German manufacture. Having been used on extensive tests, it entered service in April 1981. Unit 7080-17080-8080, delivered in October 1981, is fitted with Westinghouse Analogue braking.

In order to assist disabled passengers, one door on each side of each car was fitted with a grab handle. All units from 7082-17082-8082 onwards were fitted with them at Metro-Cammell, and those in service before unit 7082 were modified at Ealing Common. These handles recently had to be removed owing to misuse by the hooligan element of society.

An interior view of a District Line D stock car. Apart from one centre bay of transverse seats, all seats are of the longitudinal type. Capital Transport

The first train of D stock entered passenger service on Monday 28th January 1980.

DM 7108 of unit 7108-17108-8108 was delivered in June 1982 with experimental ventilation equipment, including grilles over the car windows, pull-down quarter lights, except at door pockets, and additional slots for expelled air on the car roof. Following the testing of this equipment it was decided that all D stock trains should be modified similarly, but without the grilles above the windows. The prototype unit returned to Metro-Cammell in October 1982, being modified and returned with the last unit of D stock (8129-17129-7129) on 29th June 1983 – exactly four years from the delivery of the very first unit. The 20 double-cab units of D stock were modified at Acton Works between March 1983 and June 1984, whereas the single-cab units were returned to Metro-Cammell at Birmingham in pairs from March 1983, the last to be received back in modified condition being units 7080 and 7059 in January 1985. DM 7108, although now the same as all the other modified units, remains distinguishable as the prototype in that the grilles over the car windows have been panelled over.

With service reductions having taken place on most Underground lines from December 1982, and ventilation modifications being completed in January 1985, there was ample spare D stock available to provide the service on the Metropolitan East London Line, allowing displaced A60/62 stock to form a float for OPO conversion. Double-cab units of D stock took over on the East London Line from 27th April 1985, initially as crew-operated trains, but OPO from 13th May 1985.

With the subsequent need to increase the District Line service, and with the A stock OPO conversion completed, the latter returned to the Metropolitan East London Line in May 1987, the complete D stock fleet now operating on the District main line.

ENGINEERS' VEHICLES

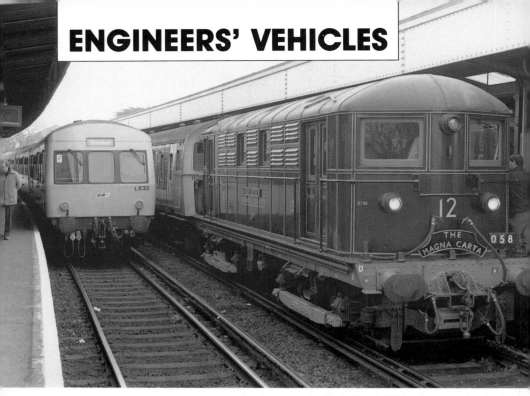

In December 1989, former Metropolitan electric locomotive No.12 (Sarah Siddons) was used to haul stock between Windsor & Eton and Staines to celebrate 125 years of the line. It is seen at the latter, next to a Metro-Cammell DMU. R.J. Greenaway

Electric locomotive No.12, named 'Sarah Siddons', was one of 20 locomotives built by Metropolitan Vickers in 1922/23 to haul compartment stock trains on the Metropolitan Line. It is now normally used as a brake block test locomotive, although during the autumns of 1977-79, No.12 was used with other service stock in leaf-clearing experiments between Rickmansworth and Amersham.

In May 1982, No.12 emerged from Acton Works after extensive overhaul painted in early LPTB livery, complete with gold lining and red window surrounds. It has since been used on a number of enthusiasts' rail tours on both London Underground and British Rail (Southern Region), being adaptable to work on the Southern Region's third-rail system.

One electric locomotive awaits disposal in Ruislip depot. Numbered L11 it was converted from two Pre-1938 stock motor cars (3080 and 3109) in 1964 for shunting stock in Acton Works, being fitted at one end with couplers at 'tube' and 'surface' stock height. It was made redundant when overhauls of stock were transferred to depots.

To replace the three remaining steam locomotives in 1971, three Sentinel diesel hydraulic locomotives with Rolls-Royce engines were received by London Transport, secondhand. They were numbered DL81, DL82 and DL83 by LT and were built in 1967 (DL82 and DL83) and 1968 (DL81) by Rolls-Royce Ltd of Shrewsbury and were purchased from Thomas Hill of Rotherham. They are used for shunting in Neasden and Lillie Bridge depots. Permanently coupled to each locomotive is a bogie tender, numbered DT81, DT82 and DT83. These were built from bogies of withdrawn Q stock and were necessary to operate some track circuits, the diesel locomotives being unable to do so on their own. Sleet brushes attached to the beams on the tenders are fitted to clear snow and ice from current rails. The livery of the diesel locomotives was the original 1967/68 green, with the addition of 'London Transport' transfers and locomotive numbers. DL83 was repainted in 1979, but in pea green livery. DL81 followed suit in 1980 and DL82 in 1984.

Battery locomotives are fitted with driving cabs at each end and all are similar in size to tube stock cars. They are able to operate direct from traction current or by battery power and are used to operate engineers' trains, mainly during non-traffic hours. At each end of the locomotives there is a pair of large buffers on hinges, which, on the older locomotives, can swing back if required to couple to cars of tube stock size.

There are seven different batches of locomotives, which are summarised as follows in order of age:

L35-43 were built in 1938 by the Gloucester Railway Carriage & Wagon Co. L41-43 were fitted with Metadyne equipment until withdrawal. L41 and L42 were scrapped in September 1978 and L43 in January 1980. L37 and L39 are currently withdrawn from service.

L55-61 were built by Pickering & Co; L55-60 in 1951 and L61 in 1952, and were fitted with more batteries than the previous batch. L57 was scrapped in June 1987.

L33 was built at Acton Works in 1962 and originally numbered L76. It was renumbered L33 in 1974 to conform with the numbering of other battery locomotives and is similar in construction to L55-61. L33 is currently stored in Ruislip depot, withdrawn.

L20-32 were built in 1964 by Metro-Cammell. Locomotive L25-32 were additionally fitted with cab signalling for operating on the Victoria Line, but this equipment has now been removed.

L15-19 were constructed in 1969 by Metro-Cammell and are similar to L20-24.

L44-54 were constructed in 1973 by British Rail Engineering Ltd at Doncaster.

Between September 1985 and February 1986, six new battery locomotives built by Metro-Cammell of Birmingham were delivered to supplement the existing fleet. Numbered L62-67, the new locomotives have buck-eye couplers, retractable buffers and better arrangements for battery charging and removal.

All locomotives built since 1964 are fitted with two compressors so that they can work singly if necessary. In recent years, some locomotives have been fitted with sleet brushes and all of the 1938-73 types now have rainstrips over the side cab doors. The livery of battery locomotives is now yellow, although L36 retains its maroon sides, and L44 was given green sides in July 1990.

As an experiment, L18 and L38 were fitted with buckeye couplers at Acton Works early in 1980. Following their success, all locomotives built since 1964 have been so equipped at both ends, including a small number of the earlier locomotives, at one end only.

During 1939 and 1940 eighteen tube-size sleet locomotives were constructed in Acton Works, each one being formed of two 1903 ex-Central London Railway driving motor cars placed back to back to form a double-ended locomotive. The de-icing equipment fluid is situated immediately above, inside the middle of the car. Of the original 18 converted tube cars (numbered ESL100-ESL117) only two remain, ESL107 and ESL117, both being out of service and stored withdrawn.

To transfer individual cars of tube stock between depots, pilot motor cars are utilised. Originally, eight pre-1938 stock DMs were transferred to the service stock fleet in February 1967. Four were renumbered (L130/1 in September 1967 and L134/5 in July 1968) whilst the other four were withdrawn during 1970 and 1971. L130/1 (now withdrawn) were repainted yellow in late-1982, as were L134/5 in April 1983.

The conversion of additional ballast motors from withdrawn 1938 tube stock DMs started in 1973, when four cars were converted (L140-3). L144/5 were converted in 1975, L146/7 in 1976, L148/9 in 1977 and L150-5 in 1978. The original L140 was damaged by fire at Lillie Bridge in January 1979 and was scrapped in January 1980. Its place was taken by DM 10182, conversion of which was completed in September 1980 in yellow livery. However, the first Ballast motor car to sport this livery was L144 in July 1980, having been repaired following collision damage. L150 and L151 are used as a permanent way weed-killing train. L150 and L151 were repainted into yellow livery in September 1983. The present weed killing equipment was fitted by Chipman's of Horsham in 1986 and liquid is sprayed from exterior pipework. The two-car train can therefore periodically be seen working on the open sections of the Underground network.

Four surface stock pilot motors were provided in 1971 from withdrawn Q38 stock motor cars 4416-19. They were renumbered L126-9 respectively in March 1972, but retained their red livery until September 1974 (L126/7) and October 1976 (L128/9). The latter pair were scrapped in January 1983 while L126/7 were repainted in the new service stock livery of yellow in February 1983. The exteriors of L126 and L127 were restored to their former glory in July 1990, being repainted back into Underground train red livery, complete with original numbers and London Transport transfers.

Headlight-modified battery locomotives L53 of 1973 origin (left) and L27 of 1964 vintage (right) both stand raised on blocks in Ruislip depot. John Gascoine

Pickering-built battery locomotive L56 leads a three-car train of 1938 stock through Stamford Brook on 11th May 1989, being transferred to Network SouthEast for service on the Isle of Wight. P.M. Bradley

1985 battery locomotive L65, built by Metro-Cammell, is seen in Ruislip depot. R.J. Greenaway

One of two operative pairs of 1938 stock ballast motors is L146 and L147, seen here at South Ealing with the tube stock gauging car.
David Rowe

The only pair of Pre-1938 stock pilot motors in use is L134 and L135 seen here in Ealing Common depot. L134, which is of 1927 origin, still retains the centre door pillar between the double doors.
R.J. Greenaway

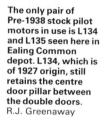

The three-car Track Recording unit is seen at Edgware on the Northern Line.
R.J. Waterhouse

Q38 pilot cars L126/7 have been repainted back into red livery and renumbered back to 4416/7. DM 4416 (ex-L126) poses at Upminster depot on the open day on 5th August 1990. R.J. Waterhouse

On 20th October 1982 a Unimog vehicle was delivered to London Transport for leaf clearing during each autumn between Amersham and Rickmansworth on the Metropolitan Line. It has separate wheels for either road or rail operation and has a Mercedes-Benz six-cylinder diesel engine with eight-speed reversing gearbox and has an attachment at the rear for removing leaves from the track. The two-unit vehicle is numbered TMM774/5 and has the road registration number of A723LNW. It is normally only used during the leaf-fall season but took part in test runs on the tunnel sections of the District and Circle lines in early 1986.

Following the demonstration at Acton Works and Lillie Bridge in January 1983 of a Unimog road/rail vehicle for shunting in depots, one such vehicle was delivered to Ealing Common depot on 18th November 1983. It has the service stock number of L84 and is registered for road use as A456NWX. A second one followed on 8th April 1986 and is numbered L85 (C622EWT).

Mercedes Benz Unimog L84 shunting in Lillie Bridge depot, which is being rebuilt. R.J. Greenaway

In addition to the locomotives there are many different types of vehicles, some with specialised equipment, which are necessary in the maintenance of the London Underground system.

There were originally seven trailers of Pre-1938 tube stock converted between 1965 and 1972 as personnel carriers, to carry staff engaged in working engineering trains. These were numbered PC850-PC856. Some personnel carriers were fitted with interior storage heaters, recognised by the shoe beam and collector shoes on one bogie. There are currently three of these cars in stock, two of which are awaiting disposal. Three additional personnel carriers were converted from withdrawn 1938 tube stock DMs in 1980-81. The three converted cars (PC857-859) were formerly DMs 11247, 11165 and 10165 respectively.

For checking clearances in tube tunnels over the London Underground railway network, there is a specially converted gauging car. Numbered G663, it was originally a 1931 Piccadilly Line trailer car built by Birmingham. It was converted to its present form at Acton in 1963. The tube gauging car G663 can be fitted with templates to surface stock loading gauge, as required, for gauging on the District and Metropolitan lines. In 1981, G663 was overhauled and repainted yellow.

Until mid-1977 London Transport used four-car 1960 stock unit 3910-4902-4903-3911 as a track recording unit, having been officially transferred to the service stock fleet in 1971. It was intended that the two Pre-1938 stock trailers should be replaced by a converted 1938 stock trailer, and to that end 012331 was converted and renumbered TRC912 in 1978. DMs 3910/1 were subsequently scrapped and TRC912 has never fulfilled its intended role, it now being a stores vehicle at Ealing Common. In the interim period, track recording has been performed by a variety of stocks, including vehicles loaned from British Rail. However, the need to regularly monitor the track condition over the whole of the Underground system resulted in a purpose-built track recording train being constructed. The actual track recording car comprises a 1973 stock trailer car (formerly 514), which was converted by BREL Derby in 1986. To provide the motive power for the car, two pilot motor cars were converted from withdrawn 1960 stock DMs (3901/5) also by BREL Derby in 1986. The track recording car is numbered TRC666 while the pilot motors are numbered L132 and L133. The three-car train is finished in an attractive livery of off-white above the waist and red below the waist, separated by an all-round black waist level band. Coupling between cars is by buckeye at British Rail height, enabling TRC666 to be coupled to BR vehicles if necessary. The recording equipment, which includes two computers, is located in TRC666, which also bears the BR TOPS number of DB999666.

In April 1980 three new tamping machines were delivered for Underground track maintenance, being built by Plasser Thuerer Ltd. They replaced older machines of various types and are numbered 771-773. Unlike their predecessors, 771-773 are able to operate track circuits and work under their own power to the nominated work site. However, because of the diesel engine, transfers via tunnel sections are undertaken using a battery locomotive as motive power.

One of three Plasser-Theurer ballast tamping machines purchased in 1980, seen in Ealing Common depot. John Gascoine

During 1990 the Underground's Tunnel Cleaning Train has been refurbished by Hunslet's of Leeds. TCC1 (minus numbers and Underground roundels) is seen in Ruislip depot while being prepared for return to service.
John Gascoine

The connections between TCC3 (nozzle car) and TCC4 (filter car) and along with TCC2, all three cars were specifically built for their role, whereas TCC1/5 were converted from 1938 stock motor cars 10226 and 10087 respectively.
John Gascoine

   The Tunnel Cleaning Train, built at Acton Works between 1972 and 1977, comprises a five-car unit numbered (from the west end) TCC1 to TCC5. TCC1 and TCC5 are driving motor cars rebuilt from withdrawn 1938 tube stock DM cars 10226 (TCC1) and 10087 (TCC5). The train is painted in yellow livery. Three floodlights are located on the outside of each motor car at the driving end, one above each front cab window for use when cleaning. Immediately behind the driver's cab there is a compartment for the cleaning operator. Whilst cleaning, the train is able to move only on hydraulic drive. This equipment is on TCC1 only, although it can be controlled from either cleaning compartment thus allowing cleaning to be carried out in either direction. Cars TCC2 and TCC4 are Filter cars and unload the dust into built-in containers. TCC3 is a Nozzle car which, by means of a fan, draws the dust into the Filter cars. The speeds for cleaning on hydraulic drive can be selected at ½, 1½, 4½ or 6mph. The train has worked on all tube lines and is fitted with train radio equipment. In 1990 the five-car train was refurbished by Hunslet's of Leeds, returning to Ruislip depot in July and August.
   In addition to the various types of service stock already described, there are a number of other vehicles in the Underground's service stock fleet. The majority of the older wagons have 'Ward' couplers at tube stock height to allow coupling to battery and ballast locomotives which are also built to tube gauge. In addition, the older flat wagons, rail wagons, diesel cranes (and their jib carriers), the cable drum wagons and the bogie well wagon all have pairs of swing-back buffers at one or both ends. The only service stock vehicles which have fixed buffers and screw/chain coupling are the brake vans built to main line gauge. The more modern vehicles are fitted with buckeye couplers.

The three personnel carriers converted from pre-1938 stock motor cars, including PC855 shown here, were withdrawn from service but still in stock at the time this book was prepared. Three ex-1938 stock examples remain at work.
R.J. Greenaway

The two-car weed-killing train, comprising 1938 stock ballast motors L150 and L151, passes through Earl's Court on the District Line. David Rowe

The tube stock gauging car, G663, in Ealing Common depot, was originally a 1931 trailer car from the Piccadilly Line. David Rowe

Electric Locomotives 2

No.	Type	Built	Builder	
†‡L11	Acton Works Yard Shunter	1931	Metro-Cammell	Ex Pre-1938 DMs 3080 and 3109 in 1964
12	Brake Block Test Loco	1922	Metropolitan Vickers Ltd.	Ex Met. loco No. 12 'Sarah Siddons' in 1962

†Yellow livery   ‡Awaiting scrapping

Battery Locomotives 47

No.	Deliv.	Buck-eye End	Builder	No.	Deliv.	Buck-eye End	Builder
L15	1970	A & D	Metro-Cammell	L44	1974	A & D	BREL Doncaster
L16	1970	A & D	Metro-Cammell	L45	1974	A & D	BREL Doncaster
L17	1971	A & D	Metro-Cammell	L46	1974	A & D	BREL Doncaster
L18	1971	A & D	Metro-Cammell	L47	1974	A & D	BREL Doncaster
L19	1971	A & D	Metro-Cammell	L48	1974	A & D	BREL Doncaster
L20	1964	A & D	Metro-Cammell	L49	1974	A & D	BREL Doncaster
L21	1964	A & D	Metro-Cammell	L50	1974	A & D	BREL Doncaster
L22	1965	A & D	Metro-Cammell	L51	1974	A & D	BREL Doncaster
L23	1965	A & D	Metro-Cammell	L52	1974	A & D	BREL Doncaster
L24	1965	A & D	Metro-Cammell	L53	1974	A & D	BREL Doncaster
L25	1965	A & D	Metro-Cammell	L54	1974	A & D	BREL Doncaster
L26	1965	A & D	Metro-Cammell	L55	1951		Pickering & Co.
L27	1965	A & D	Metro-Cammell	L56	1951	D	Pickering & Co.
L28	1965	A & D	Metro-Cammell	L58	1951		Pickering & Co.
L29	1965	A & D	Metro-Cammell	L59	1951		Pickering & Co.
L30	1965	A & D	Metro-Cammell	L60	1951		Pickering & Co.
L31	1965	A & D	Metro-Cammell	L61	1952	A	Pickering & Co.
L32	1965	A & D	Metro-Cammell	L62	1985	A & D	Metro-Cammell
*†L33	1962		Acton Works	L63	1985	A & D	Metro-Cammell
L35	1938		Gloucester	L64	1985	A & D	Metro-Cammell
L36	1938		Gloucester	L65	1985	A & D	Metro-Cammell
†L37	1938		Gloucester	L66	1986	A & D	Metro-Cammell
L38	1938	D	Gloucester	L67	1986	A & D	Metro-Cammell
†L39	1938	A	Gloucester				

*Built at Acton Works originally numbered L76. Renumbered L33 in 1974.
†Withdrawn
Note: Only one locomotive (L36) remains in the old livery, but has yellow ends.

Diesel Locomotives and Tenders 3

Loco No.	Built	Builder	Works No.	Tender No.
DL81	1968	Rolls-Royce, Shrewsbury	10278	DT81
DL82	1968	Rolls-Royce, Shrewsbury	10272	DT82
DL83	1967	Rolls-Royce, Shrewsbury	10271	DT83

Pea green livery

Electric Sleet Locomotives 2

No.	Location	Built	Conv.	Builder	LPTB Nos.
*†ESL107	Ruislip	1903	1939	Metro-Carriage/Birmingham	3944/3981
*†ESL117	Ruislip	1903	1940	Metro-Carriage/Birmingham	3954/3995

*Out of service   †Yellow livery

Surface Stock Pilot Motor Cars 2

No.	Built	Notes
4416	1938	Ex Q38 Stock DM 4416 in 1971 to L126.
4417	1938	Ex Q38 Stock DM 4417 in 1971 to L127.

Note: Reverted to original numbers and livery 1990.

Tube Stock Pilot Motor Cars 6

*†L130	1934	Ex-Pre-1938 Stock DM 3690 in 1967
*†L131	1934 ⎫	Ex-Pre-1938 Stock DM 3693 in 1967
L132	1960 ⎬	Ex-1960 Cravens DMs 3901/5, converted 1987 at BREL Derby
L133	1960 ⎭	to TRC pilot motors
†L134	1927	Ex-Pre-1938 Stock DM 3370 in 1968
†L135	1934	Ex-Pre-1938 Stock DM 3701 in 1968

*Withdrawn   †Yellow livery

Ballast Motor Cars 11

No.	Built	Built by	Converted	Previous No.
*‡L141	1938	Metro-Cammell	1973	11067
*‡L142	1938	Metro-Cammell	1973	10021
*‡L143	1938	Metro-Cammell	1973	10065
*‡L144	1938	Metro-Cammell	1975	10257
* L145	1938	Metro-Cammell	1975	11027
L146	1938	Metro-Cammell	1976	10034
L147	1938	Metro-Cammell	1976	11034
‡§L150	1938	Metro-Cammell	1978	†10327
‡§L151	1938	Metro-Cammell	1978	†11327
*‡L152	1938	Metro-Cammell	1978	10266
*L153	1938	Metro-Cammell	1978	11266

*Out of service   ‡Yellow livery   §Weed Killer Cars.
†These cars were originally numbered 90327 and 91327 respectively.

Four-Wheel Flat Wagons (10 tons capacity) 2

F305 BR Shildon 1964   F328 Gloucester 1935

Bogie Flat Wagons (30 tons capacity) 36

*F332	*F341	*F347	‡F357	‡F364	‡F385	F391	F398
*F333	*F342(c)	*F351(c)	‡F358	‡F366	‡F386	F393	
*F335	*F343(c)	F352	*F359	‡F369	F388	‡F394	
*F336	‡F344	‡F353	*F362	F383	F389	F396	
F340(s)	*F345(c)	F355(c)	*F363	F384	F390	F397	

Builders:	F332–340	Gloucester	1937	F383	Gloucester	1959
	F341–369	Gloucester	1951	F384–398	BR Ashford	1956

*Withdrawn from service   (c) Fitted with cement mixers, yellow livery
‡Refurbished with buck-eye couplers and retractable buffers, yellow livery
(s) Fitted with Smalley 3009 concrete breaker

Bogie Hopper Wagons (30 tons capacity) 22

Built 1981 by W.H. Davis & Sons. All are in yellow livery.

HW201	HW204	HW207	HW210	HW213	HW216	HW219	HW222
HW202	HW205	HW208	HW211	HW214	HW217	HW220	
HW203	HW206	HW209	HW212	HW215	HW218	HW221	

Rail Wagons (20 tons capacity) 33

*RW455	RW476	RW481	RW488	‡RW494	‡RW499	‡RW504
*RW457	RW477	RW483	†‡RW490	‡RW495	‡RW500	RW505
RW470	RW478	RW484	‡RW491	‡RW496	‡RW501	RW506
RW472	RW479	RW486	‡RW492	‡RW497	‡RW502	
RW473		RW487	‡RW493	‡RW498	‡RW503	

Builders:	RW455–457	Metro-Cammell	1931			
				RW476–487	Gloucester	1950
				RW488–494	Gloucester	1958
	RW470–473	Gloucester	1937	RW495–506	BR Ashford	1965

*Withdrawn from service
†Fitted with electric hoist for operating with long-rail trains
‡Fitted with handrails for operating with long-rail trains; yellow livery

Brake Vans 5

No.	Capacity	Builder	Year	No.	Capacity	Builder	Year
†B558	20 tons	Hurst Nelson	1935	§B584	20 tons	BR Ashford	1965
‡B580	20 tons	BR Ashford	1965	‡B585	20 tons	BR Ashford	1965
§B583	20 tons	BR Ashford	1965				

†Painted in maroon livery with yellow ends
‡Converted to Tube Stock Match Wagons at W.H. Davis & Sons; yellow livery
§In use as Surface Stock Match Wagons; converted in 1980. Also numbered
LTE95800/1 for BR identification purposes.

Diesel Cranes 8

No.	Builder	Built	No.	Builder	Built
†DEC617	Taylor & Hubbard	1955	†C624	Cowan & Sheldon	1984
†DEC618	Taylor & Hubbard	1956	†C625	Cowan & Sheldon	1984
DEC622	Taylor & Hubbard	1964	†C626	Cowan & Sheldon	1984
†C623	Cowan & Sheldon	1982	*†DHC627	Cowan & Sheldon	1986

†Yellow livery *Twin Jib Track Relaying Machine

Gauging Car 1

G663	Tube	Converted 1963	Ex Pre-1938 stock trailer 7131 built 1931 by Birmingham (painted yellow 1981)

Track Recording Car 1
TRC666 Converted 1987, ex 1973 stock trailer 514

Jib Carriers for cranes 2

No.	Built	Notes
JC689	1925 Cammell Laird	Ex Flat Wagon F309 in 1955
†JC691	1931 Metro-Cammell	Ex Flat Wagon F312 in 1963

†Yellow livery

Plasser-Theurer Track Maintenance Machines 3

No.	Date New	Type	
TMM771	1980	PU0716	Tamping Machine
TMM772	1980	PU0716	Tamping Machine
TMM773	1980	PU0716	Tamping Machine

Unimog Road/Rail Vehicles 3

TMM774	Motor)	1982	Leaf Clearing	A723LNW
TMM775	Trailer)			
L84	Motor	1983	Depot Shunter	A456NWX
L85	Motor	1986	Depot Shunter	C622EWT

Rail Wagons (20 tonnes capacity) 26 Built 1986 by Procor

RW801	RW805	RW809	RW813	RW817	RW821	RW825
RW802	RW806	RW810	RW814	RW818	RW822	RW826
RW803	RW807	RW811	RW815	RW819	RW823	
RW804	RW808	RW812	RW816	RW820	RW824	

Tube Stock Personnel Carriers 6

*PC850	Converted 1965 Ex Pre-1938 stock trailer 7061 built 1931 by Birmingham
*PC851	Converted 1965 Ex Pre-1938 stock trailer 7063 built 1931 by Birmingham
*‡PC855	Converted 1966 Ex Pre-1938 stock trailer 7071 built 1931 by Birmingham
‡PC857	Converted 1980 Ex 1938 stock motor car 11247 built by Metro-Cammell
‡PC858	Converted 1980 Ex 1938 stock motor car 11165 built by Metro-Cammell
‡PC859	Converted 1981 Ex 1938 stock motor car 10165 built by Metro-Cammell

‡Yellow livery   *Withdrawn

HD871, one of the six new High-Deck wagons built in 1987 by Procor, seen in Ruislip depot. Brian Hardy

High-Deck 40 tonne Wagons 6
Built 1987 by Procor

HD871	HD872	HD873	HD874	HD875	HD876

General Purpose Wagons (30 tonnes capacity) 41
Built 1985 Procor. All are in yellow livery.

GP901	GP905	GP909	GP913	GP917	GP921	GP925	GP929	GP933	GP937	GP941
*GP902	GP906	GP910	GP914	GP918	GP922	GP926	GP930	GP934	GP938	
GP903	GP907	GP911	GP915	GP919	GP923	GP927	GP931	GP935	GP939	
GP904	GP908	GP912	GP916	GP920	GP924	GP928	GP932	GP936	GP940	

*Fitted with Steiner HSM 800 Trench digger.

Cement Mixer/Match Wagons 12
Built 1987 by Procor — Operated as twin units

CM950	CM952	CM954	MW956	MW958	MW960
CM951	CM953	CM955	MW957	MW959	MW961

Bogie Well Wagon 1

*WPW1000	Built 1937	Ex Diesel Generator Wagon, 1975
*Withdrawn		

Cable Drum Wagons 3

CW1050	CW1051	CW1052	Built 1940 by Gloucester (yellow livery 1984)

Tunnel Cleaning Train 1

TCC1	Driving motor 'A' end ex 1938 stock motor car 10226	
TCC2 TCC3 TCC4 }	Cars with cleaning equipment, built at Acton Works, 1972-77	} Yellow livery
TCC5	Driving motor 'D' end ex 1938 stock motor car 10087	

Stores Vehicle 1
TRC912   Converted 1978, ex 1938 stock trailer 012331

UNIT FORMATIONS

Where units are out of service for an extended period but are likely to be returned to service, these are shown in this section in italics. Withdrawn stock is listed on page 77.

Withdrawn stock is listed on page 77.

BAKERLOO LINE

1972 MkII Stock: Four-Car Units

DM 'A' End S. Leading	Trailer	Trailer	DM 'D' End N. Middle
3231	4231	4331	3331
3232	4232	4332	3332
3233	4233	4333	3333
3234	4234	4334	3334
3235	4235	4335	3335
3236	4236	4336	3336
3237	4237	4337	3337
3238	4238	4338	3338
3239	4239	4339	3339
3240	4240	4340	3340
3241	4241	4341	3341
3242	4242	4342	3342
3243	4243	4343	3343
3244	4244	4344	3344
3245	4245	4345	3345
3246	4246	4346	3346
3247	4247	4347	3347
3248	4248	4348	3348
*3249	4249	4349	3349
3250	4250	4350	3350
3251	4251	4351	3351
3252	4252	4352(d)	3352
3253	4253	4353(d)	3353
3254	4254	4354(d)	3354
3255	4255	4355(d)	3355
*3256	4256	4356(d)	3356
3257	4257	4357(d)	3357
3258	4258	4358(d)	3358
3259	4259	4359(d)	3359
3260	4260	4360(d)	3360
3261	4261	4361(d)	3361
3262	4262	4362(d)	3362
3263	4263	4363(d)	3363

1972 MkII Stock: Three-Car Units

UNDM 'A' End S. Middle	Trailer	DM 'D' End N. Leading
3431	4531	3531
3432	4532	3532
3433	4533	3533
3434	4534	3534
3435	4535	3535
3436	4536	3536
3437	4537	3537
3438	4538	3538
3439	4539	3539
3440	4540	3540
3441	4541	3541
3442	4542	3542
*3443	4543	3543
3444	4544	3544
3445	4545	3545
3446	4546	3546
3447	4547	3547
3448	4548	3548
3449	4549	3549
3450	4550	3550
3451	4551	3551
3452	4552	3552
3453	4553	3553
3454	4554	3554
3455	4555	3555
3456	4556	3556
3457	4557	3557
*3458	4558	3558
3459	4559	3559
3460	4560	3560
3461	4561	3561
3462	4562	3562
3463	4563	3563

* First units to be refurbished, 1990

(d) Fitted with de-icing equipment.
All 'A' and 'D' end leading DMs are fitted with train radio equipment.

CENTRAL LINE

1962 Stock: Four-Car Double-Ended Units

DM 'A' End West	Trailer	NDM	DM 'D' End East	DM 'A' End West	Trailer	NDM	DM 'D' End East
1400	2400	9401	1401	1550	2550	*9551	1551
1406	2406(d)	9407	1407	1556	2556(d)	9557	1557
1410	2410	9411	1411	1560	2560	9561	1561
1420	2420	9421	1421	1570	‡2570	*9571	1571
1430	2430	9431	1431	1576	2576(d)	9577	1577
1440	2440	9441	1441	1580	‡2580	9581	1581
1450	2450	9451	1451	1590	‡2590	*9591	1591
1456	2456(d)	9457	1457	1600	‡2600	9601	1601
1460	‡2460	9461	1461	1606	2606(d)	*9607	1607
1470	2470	9471	1471	1610	2610	*9611	1611
1480	2480	9481	1481	1620	2620	9621	1621
1490	‡2490	9491	1491	1630	2630	*9631	1631
1500	‡2500	‡9501	‡1501	1640	2640	9641	1641
1506	2506(d)	9507	1507	1650	‡2650	*9651	1651
1510	‡2510	*9511	1511	1660	2660	9661	1661
1520	2520	9521	1521	1670	2670	*9671	1671
1530	2530	9531	‡1531	1680	2680	9681	1681
1540	2540	9541	1541	1690	2690	*9691	1691

1962 Stock: Four-Car 'A' End Units

DM 'A' End West Leading	Trailer	NDM	DM 'D' End East Middle
1402	2402	9403	1403
1404	2404	9405	1405
1408	‡2408	9409	1409
1412	2412	9413	1413
1414	2414	9415	1415
‡1416	2416(d)	9417	1417
1418	2418	9419	1419
1422	2422	9423	1423
1424	2424	9425	1425
1426	2426(d)	9427	1427
1428	2428	9429	1429
1432	2432	9433	1433
1434	2434	9435	1435
1436	2436(d)	9437	1437
1438	2438	9439	1439
1442	2442	9443	1443
1444	2444	9445	1445
1446	2446(d)	9447	1447
1448	‡2448	9449	1449
1452	‡2452	9453	1453
1454	2454	9455	1455
1462	‡2462	9463	1463
1464	2464	9465	1465
1466	2466(d)	9467	1467
1468	2468	9469	1469
1472	2472	9473	1473
1474	‡2474	9475	1475
1476	2476(d)	9477	1477
1478	‡2478	9479	1479
1482	2482	9483	1483
1484	2484	9485	1485
1486	2486(d)	9487	1487
1488	‡2488	9489	1489
1492	‡2492	9493	1493
1494	‡2494	9495	1495
1496	2496(d)	9497	1497
1498	2498	9499	1499
1502	2502	9503	1503
1504	‡2504	9505	1505
1508	2508	9509	1509
1512	2512	9513	1513
1514	2514	*9515	1515
1516	2516(d)	9517	1517
1518	‡2518	*9519	1519
1522	‡2522	*9523	1523
1524	‡2524	9525	1525
1526	2526(d)	*9527	1527
1528	‡2528	9529	1529
1532	‡2532	9533	1533
1534	2534	*9535	1535
1536	2536(d)	9537	1537
1538	2538	*9539	1539
1544	2544	9545	1545
1546	2546(d)	*9547	1547
1548	2548	9549	1549
1552	2552	9553	1553
1554	2554	*9555	1555
1566	2566(d)	*9567	1567
1586	2586(d)	*9587	1587
1596	2596(d)	9597	1597
1616	2616(d)	9617	1617
1626	2626(d)	*9627	1627
1636	2636(d)	9637	1637
1646	2646(d)	*9647	1647
1742	2742	9743	1743

1962 Stock: Four-Car 'D' End Units

DM 'A' End West Middle	Trailer	NDM	DM 'D' End East Leading
‡1542	‡2542	‡9543	1543
1558	2558	*9559	1559
1562	2562	*9563	1563
1564	2564	9565	1565
1568	2568	9569	1569
1572	2572	9573	1573
1574	2574	*9575	1575
1578	2578	*9579	1579
1582	‡2582	*9583	1583
1584	2584	9585	1585
1588	2588	9589	1589
1592	2592	9593	1593
1594	2594	*9595	1595
1598	2598	*9599	1599
1602	‡2602	*9603	1603
1604	2604	9605	1605
1608	‡2608	9609	1609
1612	‡2612	9613	1613
1614	2614	*9615	1615
1618	‡2618	*9619	1619
1622	2622	*9623	1623
1624	‡2624	9625	1625
1628	‡2628	9629(x)	1629
1632	‡2632	9633	1633
1634	2634	*9635	1635
1638	‡2638	*9639	1639
1642	2642	*9643	1643
1644	‡2644	9645	1645
1648	‡2648	9649	1649
1652	2652	9653	1653
1654	2654	*9655	1655
1656	2656	‡9657	1657
1662	2662	*9663	1663
1664	2664	9665	1665
1666	2666	*9667	1667
1668	2668	9669	1669
1672	2672	9673	1673
1674	‡2674	*9675	1675
1676	2676	9677	1677
1678	‡2678	*9679	1679
1682	‡2682	*9683	1683
1684	‡2684	9685	1685
1686	2686	*9687	1687
1688	2688	9689	1689
1692	‡2692	9693	1693
1694	‡2694	*9695	1695
1696	‡2696	9697	1697
1698	2698	*9699	1699
1700	‡2700	9701	1701
1702	‡2702	*9703	1703
1704	‡2704	9705	1705
1706	2706	*9707	1707
1708	2708	9709	1709
1710	2710	*9711	1711
1712	2712	9713	1713
1714	‡2714	*9715	1715
1716	2716	9717	1717
1718	‡2718	*9719	1719
1720	‡2720	9721	1721
1722	2722	*9723	1723
1724	2724	9725	1725
1726	2726	*9727	1727
1728	‡2728	9729	1729
1730	2730	*9731	1731
1734	‡2734	*9735	1735
1736	‡2736	*9737	1737
1750	2750	*‡9751	1751

*1959 stock
‡Renumbered trailers; see list on page 95 for details of the original numbers
(d) Fitted with de-icing equipment   (x) Fitted with external door-inspection hatches

1990 Stock: Two-Car Units

This stock will commence replacement of 1962 stock in 1992.

DM 'A'	NDM 'B'	DM 'A'	NDM 'B'	DM 'A'	NDM 'B'	NDM 'B'	NDM 'C'
91001	92001	91157	92157	91313	92313	92112	93112
91003	92003	91159	92159	91315	92315	92114	93114
91005	92005	91161	92161	91317	92317	92116	93116
91007	92007	91163	92163	91319	92319	92118	93118
91009	92009	91165	92165	91321	92321	92120	93120
91011	92011	91167	92167	91323	92323	92122	93122
91013	92013	91169	92169	91325	92325	92124	93124
91015	92015	91171	92171	91327	92327	92126	93126
91017	92017	91173	92173	91329	92329	92128	93128
91019	92019	91175	92175	91331	92331	92130	93130
91021	92021	91177	92177	91333	92333	92132	93132
91023	92023	91179	92179	91335	92335	92134	93134
91025	92025	91181	92181	91337	92337	92136	93136
91027	92027	91183	92183	91339	92339	92138	93138
91029	92029	91185	92185	91341	92341	92140	93140
91031	92031	91187	92187	91343	92343	92142	93142
91033	92033	91189	92189	91345	92345	92144	93144
91035	92035	91191	92191	91347	92347	92146	93146
91037	92037	91193	92193	91349	92349	92148	93148
91039	92039	91195	92195			92150	93150
91041	92041	91197	92197			92152	93152
91043	92043	91199	92199	NDM 'B'	NDM 'C'	92154	93154
91045	92045	91201	92201			92156	93156
91047	92047	91203	92203	92002	93002	92158	93158
91049	92049	91205	92205	92004	93004	92160	93160
91051	92051	91207	92207	92006	93006	92162	93162
91053	92053	91209	92209	92008	93008	92164	93164
91055	92055	91211	92211	92010	93010	92166	93166
91057	92057	91213	92213	92012	93012	92168	93168
91059	92059	91215	92215	92014	93014	92170	93170
91061	92061	91217	92217	92016	93016	92172	93172
91063	92063	91219	92219	92018	93018	92174	93174
91065	92065	91221	92221	92020	93020	92176	93176
91067	92067	91223	92223	92022	93022	92178	93178
91069	92069	91225	92225	92024	93024	92180	93180
91071	92071	91227	92227	92026	93026	92182	93182
91073	92073	91229	92229	92028	93028	92184	93184
91075	92075	91231	92231	92030	93030	92186	93186
91077	92077	91233	92233	92032	93032	92188	93188
91079	92079	91235	92235	92034	93034	92190	93190
91081	92081	91237	92237	92036	93036	92192	93192
91083	92083	91239	92239	92038	93038	92194	93194
91085	92085	91241	92241	92040	93040	92196	93196
91087	92087	91243	92243	92042	93042	92198	93198
91089	92089	91245	92245	92044	93044	92200	93200
91091	92091	91247	92247	92046	93046	92202	93202
91093	92093	91249	92249	92048	93048	92204	93204
91095	92095	91251	92251	92050	93050	92206	93206
91097	92097	91253	92253	92052	93052	92208	93208
91099	92099	91255	92255	92054	93054	92210	93210
91101	92101	91257	92257	92056	93056	92212	93212
91103	92103	91259	92259	92058	93058	92214	93214
91105	92105	91261	92261	92060	93060	92216	93216
91107	92107	91263	92263	92062	93062	92218	93218
91109	92109	91265	92265	92064	93064	92220	93220
91111	92111	91267	92267	92066	93066	92222	93222
91113	92113	91269	92269	92068	93068	92224	93224
91115	92115	91271	92271	92070	93070	92226	93226
91117	92117	91273	92273	92072	93072	92228	93228
91119	92119	91275	92275	92074	93074	92230	93230
91121	92121	91277	92277	92076	93076	92232	93232
91123	92123	91279	92279	92078	93078	92234	93234
91125	92125	91281	92281	92080	93080	92236	93236
91127	92127	91283	92283	92082	93082	92238	93238
91129	92129	91285	92285	92084	93084	92240	93240
91131	92131	91287	92287	92086	93086	92242	93242
91133	92133	91289	92289	92088	93088	92244	93244
91135	92135	91291	92291	92090	93090	92246	93246
91137	92137	91293	92293	92092	93092	92248	93248
91139	92139	91295	92295	92094	93094	92250	93250
91141	92141	91297	92297	92096	93096	92252	93252
91143	92143	91299	92299	92098	93098	92254	93254
91145	92145	91301	92301	92100	93100	92256	93256
91147	92147	91303	92303	92102	93102	92258	93258
91149	92149	91305	92305	92104	93104	92260	93260
91151	92151	91307	92307	92106	93106	92262	93262
91153	92153	91309	92309	92108	93108	92264	93264
91155	92155	91311	92311	92110	93110	92266	93266

1990 Stock: Two-Car De-icing Units

Non Driving Motor 'B'	Non Driving Motor 'C'	Non Driving Motor 'B'	Non Driving Motor 'C'	Non Driving Motor 'B'	Non Driving Motor 'C'	Non Driving Motor 'B'	Non Driving Motor 'C'
92402	93402	92418	93418	92434	93434	92450	93450
92404	93404	92420	93420	92436	93436	92452	93452
92406	93406	92422	93422	92438	93438	92454	93454
92408	93408	92424	93424	92440	93440	92456	93456
92410	93410	92426	93426	92442	93442	92458	93458
92412	93412	92428	93428	92444	93444	92460	93460
92414	93414	92430	93430	92446	93446	92462	93462
92416	93416	92432	93432	92448	93448	92464	93464

1960 Stock: Three-Car OPO Units

DM 'A' End West	Trailer	DM 'D' End East
3902	4929(d)	3903
3906	4927(d)	3907
3908	4921(d)	3909

(d) Fitted with de-icing equipment.

JUBILEE LINE

1983 Stock (Batch I): Three-Car Units

DM 'A' End North	Trailer	DM 'D' End South	DM 'A' End North	Trailer	DM 'D' End South	DM 'A' End North	Trailer	DM 'D' End South
3601	4601	3701	*3611	4611	*3711	3621	4621	3721
3602	4602	3702	*3612	4612	*3712	3622	4622	3722
3603	4603	3703	3613	4613	3713	3623	4623	3723
3604	4604	3704	3614	4614	3714	3624	4624	3724
3605	4605	3705	3615	4615	3715	3625	4625(d)	3725
3606	4606	3706	3616	4616	3716	3626	4626(d)	3726
*3607	4607	*3707	3617	4617	3717	3627	4627(d)	3727
3608	4608	3708	†3618	4618	3718	3628	4628(d)	3728
*3609	4609	*3709	3619	4619	3719	3629	4629(d)	3729
*3610	4610	*3710	3620	4620	3720	3630	4630(d)	3730

*Car retains original style front vents
†Car fitted with humidity sensors

1983 Stock (Batch II): Three-Car Units

DM 'A' End North	Trailer	DM 'D' End South	DM 'A' End North	Trailer	DM 'D' End South	DM 'A' End North	Trailer	DM 'D' End South
3631	4631(d)	3731	3642	4642	3742	3653	4653	3753
3632	4632(d)	3732	3643	4643	3743	3654	4654	3754
3633	4633(d)	3733	3644	4644	3744	3655	4655	3755
3634	4634(d)	3734	3645	4645	3745	3656	4656	3756
3635	4635(d)	3735	3646	4646	3746	3657	4657	3757
3636	4636	3736	3647	4647	3747	3658	4658	3758
3637	4637	3737	3648	4648	3748	3659	4659	3759
3638	4638	3738	3649	4649	3749	3660	4660	3760
3639	4639	3739	3650	4650	3750	3661	4661	3761
3640	4640	3740	3651	4651	3751	3662	4662	3762
3641	4641	3741	3652	4652	3752	3663	4663	3763

All DMs are fitted with train radio.
(d) Fitted with de-icing equipment.

1956 Stock: Four-Car 'A' End Units

DM 'A' End N. Leading	Trailer	NDM	DM 'D' End S. Middle
1000(u)	2000(u)	9001	1001
1004	2004	9005	1005
1008	2008	9009	1009

1956 Stock: Three-Car 'D' End Units

DM 'A' End N. Middle	Trailer	DM 'D' End S. Leading
1002	2002	1003
1006	2006	1007
1010	2010	1011

1962 Stock: Four-Car 'A' End Units

DM 'A' End N. Leading	Trailer	NDM	DM 'D' End S. Middle
1742	2742	9743	1743
1744	2744	9745	1745

1962 Stock: Three-Car 'D' End Units

DM 'A' End N. Middle	Trailer	DM 'D' End S. Leading
1740	2740	1741
1746	2746	1747
1748	2748	1749

1959 Stock: Four-Car 'A' End Units

DM 'A' End N. Leading	Trailer	NDM	DM 'D' End S. Middle	DM 'A' End N. Leading	Trailer	NDM	DM 'D' End S. Middle
1012	2012	9013	1013	1180	2180(d)	9181	1181
1016	2016	9017	1017	1184	2184(d)	9185	1185
1020	2020(s)	9021(w)	1021	1188	2188(d)	9189	1189
1024	2024	9025	1025	1192	2192(d)	9193	1193
1028	2028	9029	1029	1196	2196(d)	9197	1197
1032	2032	9033	1033	1200	2200(d)	9201	1201
1036	2036(h)	9037	1037	1204	2204(d)	9205	1205
1040	2040	9041	1041	1208	2208(d)	9209	1209
1044	2044	9045	1045(p)	1212	2212(d)	9213	1213
1048	2048	9049	1049	1216	2216(d)	9217	1217
1056	2056	9057	1057	1220	2220	9221	1221
1060	2060	9061	1061	1224	2224	9225	1225
1064	2064	9065	1065	1228	2228	9229	1229
1068	2068	9069	1069	1232	2232	9232	1232
1072	2072	9073	1073	1236	2236	9237	1237
1076	2076	9077	1077	1240	2240	9241	1241
1080	2080	9081	1081	1244	2244	9245	1245
1084	2084	9085	1053	1248	2248	9249	1249
1088	2088	9089	1089	1252	2252	9253	1253
1092	2092	9093	1093	1256	2256	9257	1257
1096	2096	9097	1097	1260	2260	9261	1261
1100	2100(d)	9101	1101	1264	2264	9265	1265
1104	2104(d)	9105	1105	1268	2268	9269	1269
1108	2108(d)	9109	1109	1272	2272	9273	1273
1112	2112(d)	9113	1113	1276	2276	9277	1277
1116	2116(d)	9117	1117	1280	2280	9281	1281
1120	2120(d)	9121	1121	1284	2284	9285	1285
1124	2124(d)	9125	1125	1288	2288	9289	1289
1128	2128(d)	9129	1129	1292	2292	9293	1293
1132	2132(d)	9133	1133	1296	2296	9297	1297
1136	2136(d)	9137	1137	1300	2300	9301	1301
1140	2140(d)	9141	1141	1304	2304	9305	1305
1144	2144(d)	9145	1145	1308	2308	9309	*1309R
1148	2148(d)	9149	1149	1312	2312	9313	1313
1152	2152(d)	9153	1153				
1156	2156(d)	9157	1157				
1160	2160(d)	9161	1161				
1164	2164(d)	9165	1165				
1168	2168(d)	9169	1169				
1172	2172(d)	9173	1173				
1176	2176(d)	9177	1177				

1959 Stock: Three-Car 'D' Units

DM 'A' End N. Middle	Trailer	DM 'D' End S. Leading	DM 'A' End N. Middle	Trailer	DM 'D' End S. Leading	DM 'A' End N. Middle	Trailer	DM 'D' End S. Leading
1014	2014	1015	1118	2118	1119	1218	2218	1219
1018	2018	1019	1122	2122	1123	1222	2222	1223
1022	2022	1023	1126	2126	1127	1226	2226	1227
1026	2026	1027	1130	2130	1131	1230	2230	1231
1030	2030	*1031(p)	1134	2134	1135	1234	2234	1235
1034	2034	1035	1138	2138	1139	1238	2238	1239
1038	2038	1039	1142	2142	1143	1242	2242	1243
1042	2042	1043	1146	2146	1147	1246	2246	1247
1046	2046	1047	1150	2150	1151	1250	2250	1251
1050	2050	1051	1154	2154	1155	1254	2254	1255
1054	2054(h)	1055	1158	2158	1159	1258	2258	1259
1058	2058	1059	1162	2162	1163	1262	2262	1263
1062	2062	1063	1166	2166	1167	1266	2266	1267
1066	2066	1067	1170	2170	1171	1270	2270	1271
1074	2074	1075	1174	2174	1175	1274	2274	1275
1078	2078	1079	1178	2178	1179	1278	2278	1279
1082	2082	1083	1182	2182	1183	1282	2282	1283
1086	2086	1087	1186	2186	1187	1286	2286	1287
1090	2090	1091	1190	2190	1191	1290	2290	1291
1094	2094	1095	1194	2194	1195	1294	2294	1295
1098	2098	1099	1198	2198	1199	1298	2298	1299
1102	2102	1103	1202	2202	1203	1302	2302	1303
1106	2106	1107	1206	2206	1207	1306	2306	1307
1110	2110(h)	1111	1210	2210	1211	1310	2310	1311
1114	2114	1115	1214	2214	1215	1314	2314	1315

1972 MkI Stock: Three-Car Units

UNDM 'A' End North Middle	Trailer	DM 'D' End South Leading	UNDM 'A' End Middle North	Trailer	DM 'D' End South Leading	UNDM 'A' End Middle North	Trailer	DM 'D' End South Leading
3401	4501	3501	3410	4510	3510	3421	4521	3521
3402	4502	3502	3411	4511	3511	3422	4522	3522(a)
3403	4503	3503	3412	4512	3512	3423	4523	3523(a)
3404	4504	3504	3413	4513	3513	3424	4524	3524
3405	4505	3505	3414	4514	3514	3425	4525	3525
3406	4506	3506	3415	4515	3515	3426	4526	3526
3407	4507	3507	3417	4517(v)	3517	3428	4528	3528
3408	4508	3508	3418	4518	3518(a)	3430	4530	3530
3409	4509	3509	3419	4519	3519			

1972 MkI Stock: Four-Car Units

DM 'A' End N. Leading	Trailer	Trailer	DM 'D' End S. Middle	DM 'A' End N. Leading	Trailer	Trailer	DM 'D' End S. Middle	DM 'A' End N. Leading	Trailer	Trailer	DM 'D' End S. Middle
3201	4201	4301	3301	3210	4210	4310	3310	3221	4221	4321	3321
3202	4202	4302	3302(a)	3211	4211	4311	3311	3222	4222	4322	3322
3203	4203	4303	3303	3212	4212	4312	3312	3224	4224	4324	3324
3204	4204	4304	3304(a)	3213	4213	4313	3313	3226	4226	4326	3326
3205	4205(t)	4330	3305	3214	4214	4314	3314	3227	4227	4327	3327(a)
3206	4206	4306	3306	3215	4215	4315	3315	3228	4228	4328	3328
3207	4207	4307	3307	3218	4218	4318	3318	3229	4229	4329	3329
3208	4208	4308	3308	3219	4219	4319	3319	3230	4230	4305	3330
3209	4209	4309	3309								

*1031 originally 1085; 1309R originally 1070
(a) Painted units; see text for details`
(d) Fitted with de-icing equipment
(h) Fitted with thermostatically-controlled heaters
(p) Painted in 1920s livery, exterior and interior
(s) Silver-painted car roof
(t) Floor fitted with Dunlop tiles
(u) Unpainted car roof
(v) Floor fitted with Vamac tiles
(w) White-painted car roof
'A' end DMs of four-car units, 'D' end DMs of three-car units and all 1972 stock 32xx and 35xx DMs are fitted with train radio equipment.

1973 Stock: Three-Car Units

DM 'A' End West Leading	Trailer	UNDM
100	500	300
102	502	302
104	504	304
106	506	306
108	508	308
110	510	310
112	512	312
116	516	316
118	518	318
120	520	320
122	522	322
124	524	324
126	526	326
128	528	328
130	530	330
132	532	332
134	534	334
136	536(k)	336
138	538	338
140	540	340
142	542	342
144	544	344
146	546	346
148	548	348
150	550	350
152	552	352
154	554	354
156	556	356
158	558	358
160	560	360
162	562	362
164	564	364
166	566	366
168	568	368
170	570	370
172	572	372
174	574	374
176	576	376
178	578	378
180	580	380
182	582	382
184	584	384
186	586	386
188	588	388
190	590	390
192	592	392

DM 'A' End West Leading	Trailer	UNDM
194	594	394
196	596	396
198	598	398
200	600	400
202	602	402
204	604(d)	404
206	606(d)	406
*208	608(d)	408
210	610(d)	410
212	612(d)	412
214	614(d)	414
216	616(d)	416
218	618(d)	418
220	620(d)	420
222	622(d)	422
224	624(d)	424
226	626(d)	426
228	628(d)	428
230	630(d)	430
232	632(d)	432
234	634(d)	434
236	636(d)	436
238	638(d)	438
240	640(d)	440
242	642(d)	442
244	644(d)	444
246	646(d)	446
248	648(d)	448
250	650(d)	450
252	652(d)	452

UNDM	Trailer	DM 'D' End East Leading
301	501	101
303	503	103
305	505	105
307	507	107
309	509	109
311	511	111
313	513	113
315	515	115
317	517	117
319	519	119

UNDM	Trailer	DM 'D' End East Leading
321	521	121
323	523	123
325	525	125
327	527	127
329	529	129
331	531	131
333	533	133
335	535	135
337	537	137
339	539	139
341	541	141
343	543	143
345	545	145
347	547	147
349	549	149
351	551	151
353	553	153
355	555	155
357	557	157
359	559	159
361	561	161
363	563	163
365	565	165
367	567	167
369	569	169
371	571	171
373	573	173
375	575	175
377	577	177
379	579	179
381	581	181
383	583	183
385	585	185
387	587	187
389	589	189
391	591	191
393	593	193
395	595	195
397	597	197
399	599	199
401	601	201
403	603	203
405	605	205
407	607	207
409	609	209
411	611	211

UNDM	Trailer	DM 'D' End East Leading
413	613	213
415	615	215
417	617	217
419	619	219
421	621	221
423	623	223
425	625	225
427	627	227
429	629	229
431	631	231
433	633	233
435	635	235
437	637	237
439	639	239
441	641	241
443	643	243
445	645	245
447	647	247
449	649	249
451	651	251
453	653	253

DM 'A' End West	Trailer	DM 'D' End East
114	688	889
854	654	855
856	656	857
858	658	859
860	660	861
862	662	863
864	664	865
866	666	867
868	668	869
870	670	871
872	672	873
874	674	875
876	676	877
878	678	879
880	680	881
882	†682	883
884	684	885
886	686	887
890	690	891
§892	692	893
‡894	694	895

*Fitted with prototype 1983 stock bogies
†Fitted with experimental disc brakes
‡Unit formerly GEC ETT, now standard with Davies & Metcalfe braking
§Unit formerly Westinghouse ETT.
(d) Fitted with de-icing equipment
(k) Fitted with Kawasaki experimental bogies as prototypes for 1990 Central Line stock

All DMs are fitted with train radio equipment

1967 Stock: Four-Car 'A' end Units

DM 'A' End North	Trailer	Trailer	DM 'D' End South Middle
3001	4001	†4101	†3101
3003	4003	†4103	†3103
3005	4005	†4105	†3105
3007	4007	†4107	†3107
3009	4009	4109	3109
3011	4011	4111	3111
3012	4012	4112	3112
3016	4016	4116	3116
3017	4017	4117	3117
3018	4018	4118	3118
3020	4020	4120	3120
3022	4022	†4122	†3122
3024	4024	4124	3124
3026	4026	4126	3126
3028	4028	4128	3128
3029	4029	4129	3129
3030	4030	4130	3130
3034	4034	4134	3134
3035	4035	4135	3135
3036	4036	4136	3136
3037	4037	4137	3137
3041	4041	†4141	†3141
3042	4042	4142	3142
3043	4043	4143	3143
3045	4045	4145	3145
3046	4046	4146	3146
3047	4047	4147	3147
3048	4048	4148	3148
3050	4050	4150	3150
3052	4052	†4152	†3152
3054	4054	4154	3154
3056	4056	4156	3156

1967 Stock: Four-Car 'D' end Units

DM 'A' End North Middle	Trailer	Trailer	DM 'D' End South
3002	4002	4102	3102
3004	4004	4104	3104
3006	4006	4106	3106
3008	4008	4108	3108
3010	4010	4110	3110(p)
3013	4013	4113	3113
3014	4014	4114	3114
3015	4015	4115	3115
3019	4019	4119	3119
3021	4021	4121	3121
3023	4023	4123	3123
3025	4025	4125	3125
3027	4027	4127	3127
3031	4031	4131	3131
3032	4032	4132	3132
3033	4033	4133	3133
3038	4038	4138	3138
3039	4039	4139	3139
3040	4040	4140	3140
3044	4044	4144	3144
3049	4049	4149	3149
3051	4051	4151	3151
3053	4053	4153	3153
3055	4055	4155	3155
3057	4057	4157	3157
†3080	†4080	†4180	†3180
†3081	†4081	†4181	†3181
†3082	†4082	†4182	†3182
†3083	†4083	†4183	†3183
†3084	†4084	†4184	†3184
†3084	†4085	†4185	†3185
†3086	†4086	†4186	†3186

1967 Stock: Four-Car Double-ended Units

DM 'A' End North	Trailer	Trailer	DM 'D' End South
3058	4058	4158	3158
3059	4059	4159	3159
3060	4060	4160	3160
3061	4061	4161	3161(p)
3062	4062	4162	3162
3063	4063	4163	3163
3064	4064	4164	3164
3065	4065	4165	3165
3066	4066	4166	3166
3067	4067	4167	3167
3068	4068	4168	3168

DM 'A' End North	Trailer	Trailer	DM 'D' End South
3069	4069	4169	3169
3070	4070	4170	3170
3071	4071	4171	3171
3072	4072	4172	3172
3073	4073	4173	3173
3074	4074	4174	3174
3075	4075	4175	3175
3076	4076	4176	3176
3077	4077	4177	3177
3078	4078	4178	3178
3079	*4079	4179	3179

All 1967 stock is equipped for ATO.
*Body panels welded instead of riveted.
†1967/1972 conversions — see text for details
(p) Prototype refurbished units

D Stock: Three-Car Single-Cab Units

DM 'A' End West Leading	Trailer	UNDM
7000	17000(d)	8000
7002	17002(d)	8002
7004	17004(d)	8004
7006	17006(d)	8006
7008	17008(d)	8008
7010	17010(d)	8010
7012	17012(d)	8012
7014	17014(d)	8014
7016	17016(d)	8016
7018	17018(d)	8018
7020	17020(d)	8020
7022	17022(d)	8022
7024	17024(d)	8024
7026	17026(d)	8026
7028	17028(d)	8028
7030	17030(d)	8030
7032	17032(d)	8032
7034	17034(d)	8034
7036	17036(d)	8036
7038	17038(d)	8038
7040	17040(d)	8040
7042	17042(d)	8042
7044	17044(d)	8044
7046	17046(d)	8046
7048	17048(d)	8048
7050	17050	8050
7052	17052	8052
7054	17054	8054
7056	17056	8056
7058	17058	8058
7060	17060	8060
7062	17062	8062
7064	17064	8064
7066	17066	8066
7068	17068	8068
7070	17070	8070
7072	17072	8072
7074	17074	8074
7076	17076	8076
7078	17078	8078
*7080	*17080	*8080
7082	17082	8082
7084	17084	8084
7086	17086	8086
7088	17088	8088

DM 'A' End West Leading	Trailer	UNDM
7090	17090	8090
7092	17092	8092
7094	17094	8094
7096	17096	8096
7098	17098	8098
7100	17100	8100
7102	17102	8102
7104	17104	8104
7106	17106	8106
7108	17108	8108
7110	17110	8110
7112	17112	8112
7114	17114	8114
7116	17116	8116
7118	17118	8118
7120	17120	8120
7122	17122	8122
7124	17124	8124
7126	17126	8126
7128·	17128	8128

UNDM	Trailer	DM 'D' End East Leading
8001	17001	7001
8003	17003	7003
8005	17005	7005
8007	17007	7007
8009	17009	7009
8011	17011	7011
8013	17013	7013
8015	17015	7015
8017	17017	7017
8019	17019	7019
8021	17021	7021
8023	17023	7023
8025	17025	7025
8027	17027	7027
8029	17029	7029
8031	17031	7031
8033	17033	7033
8035	17035	7035
8037	17037	7037
8039	17039	7039

UNDM	Trailer	DM 'D' End East Leading
8041	17041	7041
†8043	†17043	†7043
8045	17045	7045
8047	17047	7047
8049	17049	7049
8051	17051	7051
8053	17053	7053
8055	17055	7055
8057	17057	7057
8059	17059	7059
8061	17061	7061
8063	17063	7063
8065	17065	7065
8067	17067	7067
8069	17069	7069
8071	17071	7071
8073	17073	7073
8075	17075	7075
8077	17077	7077
8079	17079	7079
8081	17081	7081
8083	17083	7083
8085	17085	7085
8087	17087	7087
8089	17089	7089
8091	17091	7091
8093	17093	7093
8095	17095	7095
8097	17097	7097
8099	17099	7099
8101	17101	7101
8103	17103	7103
8105	17105	7105
8107	17107	7107
8109	17109	7109
8111	17111	7111
8113	17113	7113
8115	17115	7115
8117	17117	7117
8119	17119	7119
8121	17121	7121
8123	17123	7123
8125	17125	7125
8127	17127	7127
8129	17129	7129

*Fitted with Westinghouse analogue braking
†Fitted with Knorr-Bremse experimental brake equipment
(d) Fitted with de-icing equipment

D Stock: Three-Car Double-Cab Units

DM 'A' End West	Trailer	DM 'D' End East	DM 'A' End West	Trailer	DM 'D' End East	DM 'A' End West	Trailer	DM 'D' End East
7500	17500	7501	7514	17514	7515	7528	17528	7529
7502	17502	7503	7516	17516	7517	7530	17530	7531
7504	17504	7505	7518	17518	7519	7532	17532	7533
7506	17506	7507	7520	17520	7521	7534	17534	7535
7508	17508	7509	7522	17522	7523	7536	17536	7537
7510	17510	7511	7524	17524	7525	7538	17538	7539
7512	17512	7513	7526	17526	7527			

Notes: All D stock DMs are fitted with train radio.

CIRCLE LINE

HAMMERSMITH & CITY LINE

DISTRICT LINE WIMBLEDON TO EDGWARE ROAD SERVICE

C69 Stock: Two-Car Units

DM	Uncoupling Trailer	DM	Uncoupling Trailer	DM	Uncoupling Trailer	DM	Uncoupling Trailer
5501	6501	5528	6528	5555	6555(d)	5582	6582(r)
5502	6502	5529	6529	5556	6556(d)	5583	6583
5503	6503	5530	6530	5557	6557	5584	6584
5504	6504	5531	6531	5558	6558	†5585	6585(p)
5505	6505	5532	6532	5559	6559	5586	6586
5506	6506	5533	6533	5560	6560	5587	6587
5507	6507	5534	6534	5561	6561	5588	6588
5508	6508	5535	6535	5562	6562	5589	6589
5509	6509	5536	6536	5563	6563	5590	6590
5510	6510	5537	6537	5564	6564	5591	6591
5511	6511	5538	6538	5565	6565	5592	6592
5512	6512	5539	6539(r)	5566	6566(r)	5593	6593
5513	6513	5540	6540	‡5567	‡6567	5594	6594
5514	6514	5541	6541	5568	6568	5595	6595
5515	6515	5542	6542	5569	6569(r)	5596	6596
5516	6516	5543	6543(d)(r)	5570	6570	5597	6597
5517	6517	5544	6544(d)	5571	6571	5598	6598
5518	6518	5545	6545(d)	5572	6572	5599	6599
5519	6519	5546	6546(d)	5573	6573	5600	6600
5520	6520	5547	6547(d)	5574	6574	5601	6601
5521	6521	5548	6548(d)	5575	6575	5602	6602
5522	6522	5549	6549(d)	5576	6576	5603	6603
5523	6523	5550	6550(d)	5577	6577	5604	6604
5524	6524	5551	6551(d)	5578	6578	5605	6605
5525	6525	5552	6552(d)	5579	6579	§5606	6606
5526	6526	5553	6553(d)	5580	6580		
5527	*6527	5554	6554(d)	5581	6581		

C77 Stock: Two-Car Units

DM	Uncoupling Trailer	DM	Uncoupling Trailer	DM	Uncoupling Trailer	DM	Uncoupling Trailer
5701	6701	5710	6710	5719	6719	5728	6728
5702	6702	5711	6711	5720	6720	5729	6729
5703	6703	5712	6712	5721	6721	5730	6730
5704	6704	5713	6713	5722	6722	5731	6731
5705	6705	5714	6714	5723	6723	5732	6732
5706	6706(r)	5715	6715	5724	6724	5733	6733
5707	6707	5716	6716	5725	6725		
5708	6708	5717	6717	5726	6726(r)		
5709	6709	5718	6718	5727	6727		

*Additional grilles fitted in external ventilation slots
†C77 DM
‡Tinted glass windows
§Fitted with Kiepe electrical equipment
(d) Fitted with de-icing equipment
(p) Prototype refurbished unit by BREL Derby in 'Corporate' livery, 1989
(r) Units to be refurbished by RFS Engineering, Doncaster, 1990

All DMs are fitted with train radio equipment

A60/62 Stock Four-Car 'A' End Units

DM 'A' End North Leading	Trailer	Trailer	DM 'D' End South Middle
5000	6000	6001	5001
5002	6002	6003	5003(m)
5004	6004	6005	5005
5006	6006	6007	5007
5010	6010	6011	5011
5012	6012	6013	5013
5014	6014	6015	5015
5016	6016	6017	5017
5018	6018	6019	5019
5020	6020	6021	5021(m)
5022	6022	6023	5023
5024	6024	6025	5025
5026	6026	6027	5027
5030	6030	6031	5031
5032	6032	6033	5033
*5034	6034	6035	5035
5038	6038	6039	5039
5040	6040	6041	5041
5042	6042	6043	5043(m)
5044	6044	6045	5045(r)
5046	6046	6047	5047
5048	6048	6049	5049(m)
5050	6050	6051	5051(m)
5052	6052	6053	5053(m)
5054	6054	6055	5055
5068	6068	6069	5069(r)
5070	6070	6071	5071
5072	6072	6073	5073
5074	6074	6075	5075(r)
5076	6076	6077	5077
5078	6078	6079	5079
5080	6080	6081	5081
5082	6082	6083	5083
5084	6084	6085	5085
5086	6086	6087	5087
5124	6124	6125	5125
5126	6126	6127	5127
5128	6128	6129	5129
5130	6130	6131	5131
5132	6132	6133	5133(a)
5134	6134	6135	5135
5136	6136	6137	5137
5138	6138	6139	5139
5142	6142	6143	5143

A60/62 Stock: Four-Car 'D' End Units

DM 'A' End North Middle	Trailer	Trailer	DM 'D' End South Leading
5140	6140	6141	5141
5144	6144	6145	5145
5146	6146	6147	5147
5148	6148	6149	5149
5150	6150	6151	5151
5152	6152	6153	5153
5154	6154	6155	5155
5156	6156	6157	5157
5158	6158	6159	5159
5160	6160	6161	5161
5162	6162	6163	5163
5164	6164	6165	5165
5166	6166	6167	5167
5168	6168	6169	5169
5172	6172	6173	5173
5174	6174	6175	5175
5176	6176	6177	5177
5178	6178	6179	5179
5180	6180	6181	5181
5182	6182	6183	5183
5184	6184	6185	5185
5186	6186	6187	5187
5188	6188	6189	5189
5190	6190	6191	5191
5192	6192	6193	5193
5194	6194	6195	5195
5196	6196	6197	5197
5198	6198	6199	5199
5200	6200	6201	5201
5202	6202	6203	5203
5204	6204	6205	5205
5206	6206	6207	5207
5208(h)	6208(h)	6209	5121
5210	6210	6211	5211
5212	6212	6213	5213
5214	6214	6215	5215
5216	6216	6217	5217
†5218	6218	6219	5219
5220	6220	6221	5221
5222	6222	6223	5223
5224	6224	6225	5225
5226	6226	6227	5227
5228	6228	6229	5229
5230	6230	6231	5231

A60/62 Stock: Four-Car Double-Ended Units

DM 'A' End North	Trailer	Trailer	DM 'D' End South	DM 'A' North	Trailer	Trailer	DM 'D' End South
5056	6056	6057	5057(a)	5100	6100(d)	6101	5101
5058	6058	6059	5059(a)	5102	6102(d)	6103	5103
5060	6060	6061	5061	5104	6104(d)	6105	5105
5062	6062	6063	5063(a)	5106	6106(d)	6107	5107
5064	6064	6065	5065(a)	5108	6108(d)	6109	5109
5066	6066	6067	5067(a)	5110	6110(d)	6111	5111
5088	6088(d)	6089	5089	5112	6112(d)	6113	5113
5090	6090(d)	6091	5091	5114	6114(d)	6115	5115
5092	6092(d)	6093	5093(m)	5118	6118(d)	6119	5119
5094	6094(d)	6095	5095	5120	6120(d)	6121	5209
5096	‡6096(d)	6097	5097	5122	6122(d)	6123	5123(a)
5098	6098(d)	6099	5099	*5232	*6232	*6233	*5233(a)

*Cars renumbered – see text for details.
†Fitted with prototype D stock bogies.
§Tinted glass car windows.
(a) Painted units; see text for details.

(d) Fitted with de-icing equipment.
(h) Thermostatically-controlled car heaters.
(m) Maroon car roof.
(r) Red car roof.

CAR LAYOUTS

These are diagrammatic drawings only. All stock, with the exception of 1983 DM ends, has slightly chamfered ends. Doors are officially identified by letters as shown.

1956/59/62 Tube Stock

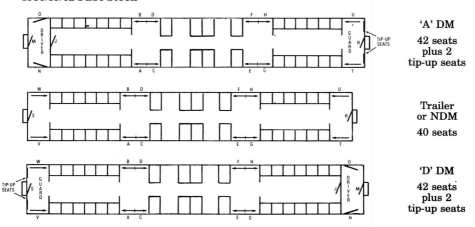

'A' DM

42 seats
plus 2
tip-up seats

Trailer
or NDM

40 seats

'D' DM

42 seats
plus 2
tip-up seats

1960/67/72 Tube Stock

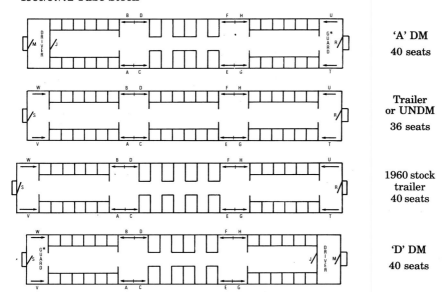

'A' DM

40 seats

Trailer
or UNDM

36 seats

1960 stock
trailer
40 seats

'D' DM

40 seats

*1972 stock, on non-ATO and OPO DMs only.

1973 Tube Stock

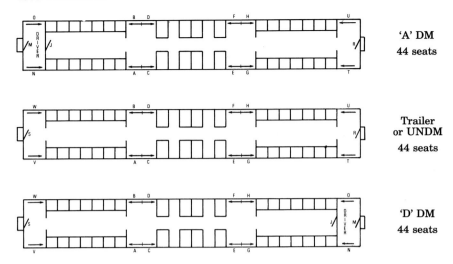

'A' DM
44 seats

Trailer
or UNDM
44 seats

'D' DM
44 seats

1983 Tube Stock

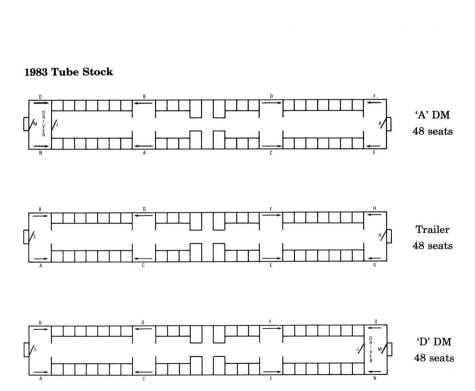

'A' DM
48 seats

Trailer
48 seats

'D' DM
48 seats

A60/62 Stock

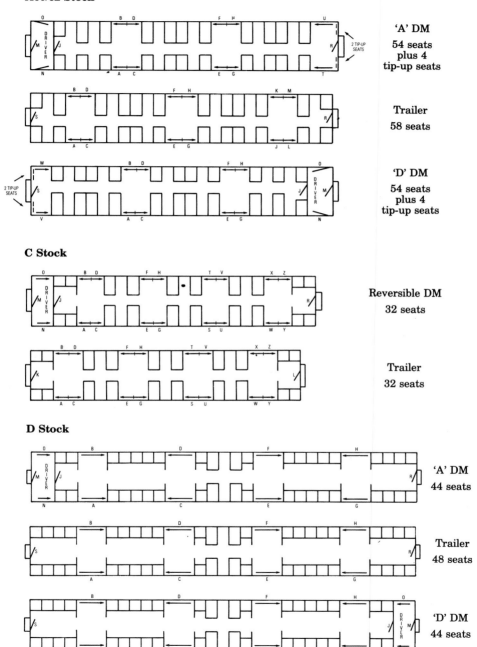

'A' DM

54 seats
plus 4
tip-up seats

Trailer

58 seats

'D' DM

54 seats
plus 4
tip-up seats

C Stock

Reversible DM

32 seats

Trailer

32 seats

D Stock

'A' DM

44 seats

Trailer

48 seats

'D' DM

44 seats

DEPOTS AND SIDINGS

Morden depot provides the greatest number of trains (38) for the Northern Line's 86-train service.
R.J. Greenaway

There are now seven main depots which maintain London's Underground rolling stock. The oldest, Ealing Common, was completed in 1905 for the District Railway electrification, and Golders Green opened in 1907 for the newly-constructed Hampstead Railway, now part of the Northern Line. Northfields was built for the Piccadilly Line western extensions and was opened in 1932. Ruislip was completed in 1939 but because of the war was not used as an Underground depot until 1948, when the western end of the Central Line extensions were opened. Neasden, originally Neasden Works of the Metropolitan Railway, was rebuilt as a depot to accommodate Metropolitan and Bakerloo Line trains by 1938. Northumberland Park was opened in 1968 for the Victoria Line ATO stock. The most modern depot in use is at Stonebridge Park, which was built specially for the Bakerloo Line when it became truncated from 1st May 1979 and the Jubilee Line was opened. From that date, Neasden depot became the home for Metropolitan and Jubilee Line trains. Overhaul and repair of Underground stock was undertaken at Acton Works, originally opened in 1922, but later greatly enlarged.

In addition a large number of subsidiary and minor depots and sidings are used to stable rolling stock: Hammersmith depot was opened in 1906 when the Hammersmith & City Line was electrified. Although regarded as a subsidiary depot of the Metropolitan Line, it is the main depot for the Hammersmith & City and Circle Line trains (and also for the District Line C77 stock), those Circle line trains entering service from Neasden depot being for stabling purposes only and not maintenance. Queens Park was opened in 1915 when the Bakerloo was extended from Paddington. It comprises two separate buildings, one south of the station where light maintenance is carried out, and one north of the station, which is used during traffic hours for reversing the service. It also contains two through tracks for the service to and from Stonebridge and Harrow & Wealdstone, connecting with the LMR tracks. Morden was opened in 1926 when what is now the Northern Line was extended from Clapham Common to Morden. Cockfosters, opened in 1932, together with Northfields replaced Lillie Bridge depot which dated from 1906. Lillie Bridge was retained as a service stock and Permanent Way depot, which it still remains. Hainault, like Ruislip, was built in 1939 but not opened until 1947 for partial use and 1948 for full use. A new depot at Upminster was opened in 1958 to replace the inadequate depot at East Ham. At the same time, nine sidings accommodating 13 trains were opened at Barking, east of the station, when major alterations to the track layout in the area separating LT and ER tracks was nearing completion.

The oldest of the minor depots are London Road (which was the main depot for the Bakerloo when it opened in 1906) and New Cross, provided when the East London Line was electrified in 1913. The shed at Wembley Park is as rebuilt in 1954 when alterations to the track layout in the area were completed, the number of 'shed' roads being reduced to five. Highgate was taken over from the LNER in 1939 (formerly Wellington carriage sidings) and additional electrified sidings (Highgate Woods) were built at the junction of the Alexandra Palace branch (Park Junction). Highgate depot was rebuilt in 1970. With the service reductions of December 1982, Highgate Wood sidings were closed, the nine trains being accommodated in the depot. However, these nine trains were subsequently transferred to other depots on the Northern Line and Highgate depot closed on 25th March 1984. The upsurge of passenger traffic, and the need for additional trains has meant that Highgate Depot will have to re-open, currently scheduled for late-1988. Two extra stabling sidings are being built at Stonebridge Park Depot and four at Northumberland Park. Edgware was built in 1924 for the extension from Golders Green. White City (formerly Wood Lane, Central London Railway) was reduced to a minor depot in 1948 when Ruislip opened.

Loughton sidings (eight, plus one adjacent to the westbound line at the station) were opened in 1948, and Woodford the previous year, both for stabling stock when the Central Line eastern extensions were opened. Two additional sidings were added at Loughton in 1963. Additional sidings at Rickmansworth, south of the station, were commissioned in 1961 for the Amersham electrification. Triangle sidings (Cromwell Curve), over which the West London Air Terminal was built in 1954, originally comprised 18 District Line and two Circle Line sidings. When the air terminal was built, the layout in the area was altered to provide five six-car and two four-car length sidings accessible only from the line between Earl's Court and High Street Kensington, unlike the original sidings which also had access to and from Gloucester Road. Only the five six-car sidings remain. The sidings at Uxbridge for Metropolitan and Piccadilly Line trains were opened in 1942. Arnos Grove sidings were opened in 1932 when the Piccadilly Line was extended from Finsbury Park, and High Barnet in 1940 when LT took over from the LNER on that branch. There are also sidings at Parsons Green, and an extra one was added in December 1958 adjacent to the westbound line between Fulham Broadway and Parsons Green. The sidings on the Piccadilly Line at South Harrow were built on the site of the former District Railway car shed, which was built for the South Harrow line electrification in 1903.

Ten new sidings at Stanmore, built on the site of the original seven (closed in June 1973), were opened for normal use in January 1977, although they had been used occasionally from mid-1976.

Modern rolling stock design and technology has reduced the amount of maintenance work required on trains, nine years between overhauls being adequate on stock built since 1967. Thus, for economic reasons, overhaul of stock has been transferred away from Acton Works, to selected depots. Acton Works, however, has a new workshop, opened in 1989, to overhaul equipment from trains. In addition, a new heavy repair shop is to be built on the high-level sidings at the east end of Ealing Common depot.

The present rolling stock overhauls are carried out as follows:

Depot & Line	Stock	From
Neasden (Metropolitan)	A60/62	Metropolitan
Golders Green (Northern)	1959	Northern
Northumberland Park (Victoria)	1967	Victoria
Cockfosters (Piccadilly)	1973	Piccadilly
Ruislip (Central)	1962	Central
Stonebridge Park (Bakerloo)	1972 MkI	Northern
Ealing Common (District)	D	District
Upminster (District)	C69/77	Circle & Hammersmith

Since the formation of the LPTB in 1933, two depots have been planned and not built and one has been built and put to other use. Aldenham Bus Overhaul Works, situated about two miles north of Edgware at the junction of the A5 and A41 roads was to have been, under the 1935-40 New Works Programme, a Northern Line depot on the proposed extension from Edgware to Bushey Heath, which was due to open in 1941, deferred by the war and afterwards abandoned. It was used as an aircraft factory during the war, becoming a temporary bus works after. It became fully equipped as a bus overhaul works in 1956, but this was closed in November 1986.

Two proposals were put forward in 1949. One was for a new depot at Stanmore to accommodate the additional trains required to operate the proposed extension of the Bakerloo Line from Elephant & Castle to Camberwell, also abandoned, and the other was for a new depot for the Piccadilly Line at Ickenham, adjacent to Ruislip depot. This also was not built.

Depot logo's applied during overhaul of rolling stock have become a common sight since the decentralisation of such work. In the first row from left to right are those for Golders Green, Stonebridge Park and Ruislip (two versions), while the second row shows Neasden, Ealing Common (a reference to the film studios), Upminster and Northumberland Park. Brian Hardy/R.J. Greenaway

DEPOTS AND SIDINGS AND TRAINS OFFERED FOR SERVICE

	BAKERLOO		CENTRAL		NORTHERN	
Main Depots	Stonebridge Park	10	West Ruislip	14	Golders Green	16
Subsidiary Depots	Queen's Park	7	Hainault (including 2 OPO)	32	Morden	40
Minor Depots	London Road	9	White City	12	Edgware Highgate	12 5
Sidings	Elephant & Castle	2	Loughton Woodford	11 6	High Barnet Golders Green Edgware	8 4 1
Totals		28		75		86

	PICCADILLY		VICTORIA		JUBILEE	
Main Depots	Northfields	25	Northumberland Park	32	Neasden	18
Subsidiary Depots	Cockfosters	31				
Sidings	South Harrow Arnos Grove Uxbridge	6 7 4	Brixton Walthamstow	2 2	Stanmore	9
Totals		73		36		27

	DISTRICT		CIRCLE/H&C		METROPOLITAN	
Main Depots	Ealing Common	29	Hammersmith	11	Neasden	20
Subsidiary Depots	Upminster	27	Neasden	5		
Minor Depots	Hammersmith	1*			Wembley Park	5
Sidings	Parsons Green Barking Triangle Sidings	8* 5 5*	Farringdon Barking Edgware Road	3 7 2	Rickmansworth Uxbridge	9 8
Platforms			Aldgate Moorgate	1 1		
Totals		75*		30		42

EAST LONDON
New Cross Depot   5

*Includes the nine C stock trains operating the Wimbledon to Edgware Road section of the District;
one at Hammersmith, five at Triangle Sidings (Cromwell Curve) and three at Parsons Green.

DOCKLANDS LIGHT RAILWAY

Car 03 of P.86 stock arrives at West India Quay. Canary Wharf takes shape in the background, which will include an expanded DLR station. R.J. Greenaway

The Docklands Light Railway now qualifies for inclusion in these pages, as from 1991 the system will be extended from east of the present terminus of Tower Gateway, in twin tube tunnels, to a new station in the City at Bank, giving interchange with LUL's Central and Northern tube lines, as well as the Waterloo & City Line of Network SouthEast. The extension to Bank was not envisaged when the original railway was conceived and for that reason, the original eleven vehicles will be unable to operate in tunnels. Subsequent builds of rolling stock have been and will be specially constructed for tunnel running conditions.

Operating at 750V dc 3rd rail (underside contact), the initial railway from Tower Gateway and Stratford to Island Gardens opened to the public on 31st August 1987, for which eleven light rail vehicles (numbered 1-11 and known as P.86 stock) were built by Linke Hofmann Busch of Salzgitter, West Germany. Each train comprises a two-body articulated unit, 28 metres long, 2.65 metres wide and 3.4 metres high, weighing 39 tonnes with a capacity for 84 seated passengers, plus 210 standing under normal standing conditions. A total of 12 of the 84 seats are longitudinal in the centre articulated section, at which position there is space for two wheelchairs. Each articulated unit has four double doorways on each side, which open and fold back inwards. The cars are finished in a striking two-tone red and blue livery, the red extending up and over the top of the doors.

Each car was shipped from Hamburg to King's Lynn and delivered by road to Poplar depot. The first car, 01, arrived on 7th August 1986, the last, 11 arriving on 30th March 1987, this vehicle having first been delivered to Debdale Park, Manchester on 9th February 1987 for light rail demonstration. Apart from unit 07, all entered passenger service on the first day of operation, 31st August 1987. Unit 07 followed on 2nd September.

The Docklands Light Railway operates entirely automatically, being computer controlled from the system headquarters at Poplar, where the depot is located. On board each train is a 'Train Captain', who is able to start the train from any doorway position. Thereafter the Train Captain is able to undertake other duties, such as ticket checking. In the event of a problem, manual driving is possible by the Train Captain using controls normally locked out of use at the outer ends of the vehicles. Difficulties with the original motorised destination blinds have seen them replaced with LCD indicators of the type fitted to later batches of stock.

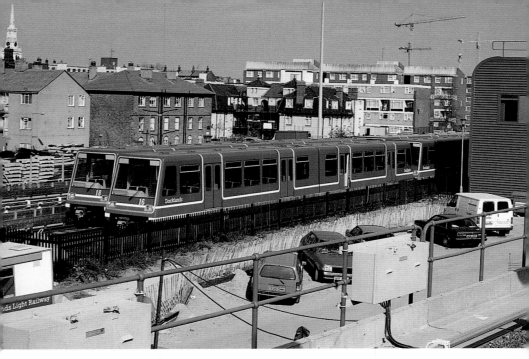

A line-up of new P.89 stock in Poplar depot on 9th April 1990, which are visually similar to their P.86 counterparts. R.J. Greenaway

The construction of the Bank extension started in March 1988 and was completed, station tunnels included, by January 1990. The work was sufficiently advanced to allow a gauging trip to and from Bank through the new tunnels on 11th July 1990 of P.86 stock unit 03, hauled by a DLR and a contractor's locomotive. In addition to the Bank extension, work is also proceeding on an eastward extension from Poplar to Beckton, where at the latter, a new depot will be built for the much extra stock required.

To meet the requirements of the future extensions, and to improve services on the initial railway, a second batch of ten cars (P.89 stock) was built by BREL of York. Numbered 12 to 21, these ten units were also delivered to Poplar depot by road from 12th December 1989 (unit 12) to 4th May 1990 (unit 21). Unit 12 entered service on 11th May 1990 and has since been joined by others, supplementing the original trains and enabling increased services to operate. The P.89 cars are very similar in appearance to their older P.86 counterparts. Although a small number of minor detail differences exist between the two types, the latter units have been built to operate in tunnel conditions.

An order for further trains has been placed with BN of Brugge in Belgium. Known as B.90 stock (25 units), B.92 stock (21 units) and B.92A stock (14 units) the general shape of the vehicles will be similar to the P.86/89 cars, but will have externally hung sliding doors and emergency communicating doors at the outer ends, as well as a new grey/red/blue interior colour scheme. There will be more handrails and in the wheelchair bay, folding seats will be provided for use when not occupied by wheelchair passengers. The first unit of B.90 stock is scheduled for delivery in January 1991.

At present, it is anticipated that one tunnel to Bank will be available for a limited DLR service from July 1991, with both tunnels available for a full service in early 1992. The Beckton extension is scheduled to open in December 1992. Fuller details of the DLR can be found in the Docklands Light Railway Official Handbook, also published by Capital Transport Publishing.

Rolling Stock as at 30th September 1990 (Cars 14/16/18/20/21 had not entered service):

P.86 Stock (LBH) 11
01 02 03 04 05 06 07 08 09 10 11

P.89 Stock (BREL) 10
12 13 14 15 16 17 18 19 20 21

WEIGHTS AND DIMENSIONS

The following is a list of the officially recorded weights, dimensions and seating capacities of each type of car in current use on the Underground. Small variations in weight occur between cars of the same basic design owing to equipment differences.

TUBE STOCK

STOCK & TYPE OF CAR		WEIGHT (Tons)	LENGTH	WIDTH	HEIGHT*	SEATS
1956	DM	26.48	52ft $2\frac{5}{16}$ins	8ft $6\frac{1}{4}$ins	9ft $5\frac{1}{2}$ins	42
	NDM	23.61	51ft $2\frac{1}{16}$ins	8ft $6\frac{1}{4}$ins	9ft $5\frac{1}{2}$ins	40
	T	20.56	51ft $2\frac{1}{16}$ins	8ft $6\frac{1}{4}$ins	9ft $5\frac{1}{2}$ins	40
1959/62	DM	26.62	52ft $2\frac{5}{16}$ins	8ft $6\frac{1}{4}$ins	9ft $5\frac{1}{2}$ins	42
	NDM	24.28	51ft $2\frac{1}{16}$ins	8ft $6\frac{1}{4}$ins	9ft $5\frac{1}{2}$ins	40
	T	20.67	51ft $2\frac{1}{16}$ins	8ft $6\frac{1}{4}$ins	9ft $5\frac{1}{2}$ins	40
1960	DM	29.89	52ft $0\frac{3}{8}$ins	8ft $6\frac{1}{4}$ins	9ft $5\frac{1}{2}$ins	40
	T (ex-1938)	20.67†	51ft $2\frac{3}{4}$ins	8ft $6\frac{1}{16}$ins	9ft $5\frac{1}{2}$ins	40
1967	DM	28.5	52ft $9\frac{1}{2}$ins	8ft 8ins	9ft $5\frac{3}{64}$ins	40
	T	19.4	52ft 5ins	8ft 8ins	9ft $5\frac{3}{64}$ins	36
1972 MkI	DM	28.2	52ft $9\frac{1}{2}$ins	8ft 8ins	9ft $5\frac{3}{64}$ins	40
	UNDM	26.8	52ft 5ins	8ft 8ins	9ft $5\frac{3}{64}$ins	40
	T	18.6	52ft 5ins	8ft 8ins	9ft $5\frac{3}{64}$ins	36
1972 MkII	DM	27.8	52ft $9\frac{1}{2}$ins	8ft 8ins	9ft $5\frac{3}{64}$ins	40
	UNDM	26.5	52ft 5ins	8ft 8ins	9ft $5\frac{3}{64}$ins	40
	T	18.1	52ft 5ins	8ft 8ins	9ft $5\frac{3}{64}$ins	36
1973	DM	27.15	57ft $3\frac{23}{32}$ins	8ft $7\frac{1}{2}$ins	9ft $5\frac{3}{64}$ins	44
	UNDM	26.16	57ft $1\frac{13}{32}$ins	8ft $7\frac{1}{2}$ins	9ft $5\frac{3}{64}$ins	44
	T	18.16	57ft $1\frac{13}{32}$ins	8ft $7\frac{1}{2}$ins	9ft $5\frac{3}{64}$ins	44
1983	DM	26.34	17226mm	2630mm	2875mm	48
	T	20.40	17676mm	2630mm	2876mm	48

SURFACE STOCK

STOCK & TYPE OF CAR		WEIGHT (Tons)	LENGTH	WIDTH	HEIGHT*	SEATS
A60/62	DM	30.8	53ft $0\frac{1}{2}$ins	9ft 8ins	12ft $1\frac{3}{32}$ins	54+4‡
	T	21.5	53ft $0\frac{1}{2}$ins	9ft 8ins	12ft $1\frac{3}{32}$ins	58
C69/77	DM	31.7	52ft 7ins	9ft 7ins	12ft 1ins	32
	T	20.2	49ft 0ins	9ft 7ins	12ft 1ins	32
D	DM	27.46	60ft $3\frac{5}{16}$ins	9ft $4\frac{7}{32}$ins	11ft $10\frac{1}{2}$ins	44
	UNDM	26.12	59ft $5\frac{13}{32}$ins	9ft $4\frac{7}{32}$ins	11ft $10\frac{1}{2}$ins	48
	T	18.41	59ft $5\frac{13}{32}$ins	9ft $4\frac{7}{32}$ins	11ft $10\frac{1}{2}$ins	48

LIGHT RAIL (DLR)

STOCK & TYPE OF CAR		WEIGHT (Tons)	LENGTH	WIDTH	HEIGHT*	SEATS
P86	Artic. Car	38.4	91ft 10ins	8ft 8ins	11ft 2ins	84
P89	Artic. Car	38.4	91ft 10ins	8ft 8ins	11ft 2ins	84

Notes: *The height is from rail level to top of the car
†Weight prior to ATO Conversion
‡Tip-up seats

STOCK OUT OF SERVICE

1938 Tube Stock
Morden Depot (stored): DMs 10012, 11012; NDM 12048; Trailer 012256.

1962 Tube Stock
Ruislip depot (for scrap): DM 1416.
Hainault depot (stored): NDM 9543.
Sandite trailer 9459 (ex-9501).

1972 MkI Tube Stock
Acton Works (upgrading prototypes): UNDMs 3420, 3429.
Acton Works (stored): UNDMs 3416, 3427.

1973 Tube Stock
Northfields depot (stored): DM 888.
Metro-Cammell (upgrading prototype): UNDM 314.

1986 Tube Stock
Neasden depot (stored): DMs 11, 12, 15, 16.
NDMs 21, 22, 25, 26.
Northfields depot (test train work): DMs 13, 14; NDMs 23, 24.

A60/62 Stock
Neasden depot (stored): Trailers 6029, 6171.
Sandite trailer 6036.

Two additional four-car double-ended A stock de-icing units are to be formed from previously stored stock. The cars are (not necessarily in the order shown, or bearing their present numbers) as follows:

5008   6008(d)   6009   5009   5036   6116(d)   6037   5037

Eight damaged/derelict A stock cars have been taken to BREL of Derby for reinstatement to service, to provide two double-ended four-car units. DM 5008 (originally 5034) is awaiting departure from Neasden. F.W. Ivey

WATERLOO & CITY LINE

Trains currently at work on the Waterloo & City Line of Network SouthEast were built in 1940 by English Electric. New stock is now on order for the replacement of these. R.J. Greenaway

The Waterloo & City Line is operated by British Rail Network SouthEast. Just over a mile in length, it operates on Mondays to Fridays until 22.00 and Saturdays until 13.30 between Bank and Waterloo, the line's only two stations, where at the latter there are stabling sidings and maintenance facilities, where most work is now undertaken.

The rolling stock operated is now over forty years old, being built in 1940 by English Electric at their Preston Works, in time for the much-needed modernisation of the line. This included changing the current rail system from the centre third rail position to the standard outside third rail position. This allowed the new stock to be tested on the Southern main line before entering service, after delivery from the makers. Modernisation was completed and the new trains entered service from 28th October 1940.

The 1940-built cars replaced the original stock, built for the opening of the line in 1898. This comprised five four-car trains built by Jackson and Sharp of the USA. A further five single motor cars were added in 1899, built by Dick Kerr, predecessors to the English Electric Company.

The order for new stock was for twelve double-ended driving motor cars (51-62), to allow single-car operation at quiet periods, and sixteen trailers (71-86), allowing five-car trains to be formed at peak periods. After the formation of British Railways on 1st January 1948 the cars were given 'S' prefix and suffix letters, although the latter, indicating the vehicle's railway of origin, was subsequently dropped. Driving motor cars seat 40 passengers and trailers seat 52. The cars were originally painted in malachite green, with aluminium ends and sliding doors, but in recent years the green has given way to BR blue. Very recent overhauls from 1980, have lost the aluminium look, in favour of off-white, and the interiors have also been restyled: Seating is now the SR standard blue and green moquette, with sliding doors and end side panels being painted in grey rather than dark blue. An indication of the stock's ancestry are the chromium-plated ventilator covers at the car ends, reading 'SOUTHERN RAILWAY', although some of these have now been replaced by covers reading 'SOUTHERN REGION'. The cars now come into British Rail's class numbering system, first introduced to BR EMU's in 1968/9, and both motors and trailers are known as Class 487.

Two DM cars (52 and 55) and three trailers (71, 79 and 82) have been withdrawn and scrapped. All surviving class 487 rolling stock on the Waterloo & City Line was repainted into Network SouthEast livery, initially sponsored by the catering firm Allied Lyons. Also, DM 57 has been modernised with fluorescent lighting and public address equipment.

The 50-year-old class 487 stock on the Waterloo & City Line is to be replaced in 1992 by stock very similar to that being built for the Central Line. Five four-car trains (ten two-car units) of 1990 stock will be built by BREL Derby.

Waterloo & City DM 57 at Waterloo main line station on Network Day in 1988. This car has been internally refurbished with fluorescent lighting and public address. R.J. Greenaway

Class 487 Stock:

Double-ended Driving Motor Cars 10

51	56	59	62
53	57*	60	
54	58	61	

*Fitted with fluorescent lighting and public address

Trailers 13

72	76	81	86
73	77	83	
74	78	84	
75	80	85	

An artist's impression of how the replacement stock for the Waterloo & City Line might look, based on the Central Line 1990 tube stock. NSE

POST OFFICE RAILWAY

Construction of the Post Office Tube railway was begun in 1915, but it was another twelve years before the first section was opened, delays having occurred because of the First World War. The first section of line opened on 5th December 1927 between Paddington and Mount Pleasant, extending eastwards to Liverpool Street on 28th December 1927, and the final section, Liverpool Street to Eastern District Office (Whitechapel), on 2nd January 1928. This non-passenger carrying railway at first conveyed only parcels, but carried letters as well from 13th February 1928. The railway is 6.44 miles in length and the 2ft gauge tracks are generally in double-track tube tunnels of nine feet in diameter, separating at station approaches into single tube tunnels of seven feet in diameter. The driverless trains operate on a centre third-rail system at either 150V dc in station areas, or at 440V dc between stations, allowing speeds of about 7mph and 35mph respectively. The automatic operation of the trains is controlled by track circuits. One of the running rails is bonded to earth and acts as a common return for both traction and track circuiting. The other rail is, electrically, a series of individual lengths insulated from each other. When the wheels of a train bridge the rails, the relay connected to that particular track circuit operates, removing power from the preceding section and not restoring it until the train has moved onto the next section. The train brakes operate in the absence of traction current, and thus the system is fail-safe. At stations, train movements are controlled manually, from a switch frame, which is mechanically and electrically interlocked. Trains can thus be shunted or routed through.

The railway generally operates for 22 hours a day — from 11.00 to 09.00, the two-hour break being utilised for routine maintenance. Major engineering and maintenance work is undertaken from 20.30 on Saturday, when the railway closes until 08.00 on Monday. On this day only it operates between 08.00 and 09.00 before resuming normal working at 11.00. During normal operations a five-minute 14-train service of one or two units is provided, supplemented as necessary with additional trains at busy times, during the evening period for example. Some express services are run between Paddington and Liverpool Street. The rolling stock is serviced and overhauled at the depot at Mount Pleasant, which is connected to the main running lines by a steeply graded incline.

For the opening of the railway, 90 four-wheel cars were built by the Kilmarnock Engineering Company with equipment by English Electric, and were designed to operate in three-car formation. These cars were not successful, and were replaced between 1930 and 1931 by 50 longer cars from English Electric, being numbered 752-763 and 793-830, the first entering service singly in May 1930. Two-car operation with these new cars commenced on 9th September 1930. A further ten similar cars (923-932) were delivered in 1936 because of increasing postal traffic. These 60 cars thus provided the daily service very reliably over the next 45 years or more. The mail containers were originally built of plywood, but after experiments with aluminium panels in 1948, the new type was adopted as standard in the 1950s.

Opposite and Above **1980 Greenbat cars in Mount Pleasant workshops, both minus containers. Car 508 is in unmodernised condition while 532 is as modernised in 1987.** R.J. Greenaway

To replace the bulk of the 1930-36 stock, 34 new cars numbered 501-534 were built by Greenbat of Leeds and were delivered to the railway at Mount Pleasant between 1980 and 1982. In addition, there are two end bogies (both numbered 535) to replace fellow motor ends when necessary. The new cars are painted in Post Office red livery, unlike their predecessors, which were in pale green. Two cars however (801 and 806) were repainted in gold livery in 1977 to celebrate the railway's Golden Jubilee.

In addition to the 34 new cars, 17 of the 1930-36 type have been retained, refurbished and subsequently returned to service, having been repainted in Post Office red livery to match the Greenbat cars. Also, one of the 1962 prototypes has been returned to service by salvaging equipment from the previously withdrawn pair. This now bears the fleet number 66.

1980 Greenbat 35

501	506	511	516	521	526	531
*502	507	512	517	522	527	*532
503	508	513	518	523	528	533
504	509	*514	519	524	529	534
505	510	515	520	525	530	†535

1930-31 English Electric 15

755	760	762	‡805	811	814	819	827
756	761	801	806	812	815	824	

1936 English Electric 2
928   931

1962 English Electric 1
66

*Rebodied 1987
†535 comprises two single motor bogies
‡805 has body ex-817 in 1981

In addition, the following cars are preserved:
601: Mount Pleasant Workshop — 1927 4-wheel stock
803: Buckingham Railway Centre, Quainton Road — 1930/1 English Electric
807: Science Museum (stored) — 1930/1 English Electric
808: Diesel & Electric Group, Minehead, Somerset — 1930/1 English Electric
809: National Railway Museum, York, — 1930/1 English Electric

Cars of 1930-36 vintage stored 24:
Western District Office: 752, 759, 763, 793, 795, 799, 802, 804, 813, 816, 818, 820, 822, 826, 830, 923, 932
Wimpole Street: 754, 797, 823, 929
Mount Pleasant: 810

1926 Battery Cars 3
1   2   3

High Holborn: 828, 930

SOLD AND PRESERVED STOCK

Unit 483.001 arrives at Brading heading south towards Shanklin. Since track rationalisation on the Isle of Wight in 1988, the line has been singled between Brading and Sandown with only the former up platform in use. David Brown

Network SouthEast Island Line (Isle of Wight)

The restricted loading gauge through Ryde tunnels on the Isle of Wight led to withdrawn Pre-1938 Tube Stock from London Underground being refurbished, for use on the remaining section of the Isle of Wight Railway between Ryde and Shanklin. A total of 43 cars were converted to standard SR third-rail operation, forming six seven-car trains with one spare DM car. Electric services on the Isle of Wight commenced on 20th March 1967. Seven-car trains were operated at busy periods, and four-car trains at other times.

Over the years the operational fleet had been gradually reduced so that by 1985 just 33 cars remained in use. In that year the stock was reformed from three/four-car sets into five-car formations and by 1987 comprised 27 cars (one two-car and five five-car units). By that time it became necessary to consider the replacement of the Pre-1938 stock, as it then varied between 53 and 64 years old according to the vehicle type. Major refurbishment would have been so costly and the hoped-for 1959/62 tube stock would not become available until the mid-1990s at the earliest. The only option therefore, was to obtain the remaining cars of 1938 stock that had themselves been given a reprieve with London Underground on the Northern Line between 1986 and 1988.

A total of 37 cars were eventually acquired from London Underground, although it was subsequently decided that formations should be in two motor car pairs, eight being required for full service. A ninth unit was proposed, but at present, this looks unlikely to be provided. The work on the selected motor cars was undertaken by BRML at Eastleigh. The cars were completely gutted and all equipment was overhauled before being put back to work. The cars were painted into Network SouthEast livery and the two-car units became 483.001-483.008. Inside, fluorescent lighting and public address were fitted, the woodwork replaced, and new flooring laid. Passenger open and close push buttons were installed. Compressors were installed on the 'D' end cars and the door controls for the guard were removed from these cars, to be operative only on 'A' end motor cars.

Interior of DM 121 of 1938 stock on the Isle of Wight, looking towards the driving cab. R.J. Greenaway

South of Ryde St John's Road, 1938 stock unit 483.001 passes Standard stock DM car 7 stabled in the long south siding. Unit 001 has the yellow front end extending around the side of the cab end. R.J. Greenaway

DM car 7 was withdrawn from service on 7th September 1990 and made its way back to Fratton on 4th October 1990, being one of five Isle of Wight Standard stock cars selected for possible restoration in London Underground style. R.J. Greenaway

The first unit (483.001) was transferred to the Isle of Wight on 5th July 1989, entering service on the Ryde Pier shuttle after a special 'launch' on 13th July. Other units followed gradually, with unit 483.008 being the last to arrive on 21st June 1990. The last unit to enter service was in fact 483.006 on 13th July 1990.

The rolling stock situation as at 30th September 1990 was as follows (all cars in Network SouthEast livery unless noted otherwise):

On Isle of Wight:
3-Car Unit

CT 'A' End North	Trailer	DM 'D' End South
28	31	5

Withdrawn class 485 cars:

Trailers	26, 27, 44, 49		DMs	2,	7

2-Car Units (Class 483) – former LUL numbers in brackets

Unit No.	DM 'A' End North	DM 'D' End South	
483.001	121 (10184)	221 (11184)	
483.002	122 (10221)	222 (11221)	
483.003/4	123 (10116)	224 (11205)	Temporary formation, out of service
483.004/3	124 (10205)	223 (11116)	Temporary formation
483.005	125 (10142)	225 (11142)	
483.006	126 (10297)	226 (11297)	
483.007	127 (10291)	227 (11291)	
483.008	128 (10255)	228 (11255)	

Class 485 stock at Fratton:

DMs		1,	3,	4,	6,	8,	9,	10,	11
Trailers		S92*	93,	94,	95				
Trailers (ex-CTs):		29,	32,	33,	34				

Class 485 stock at Strawberry Hill:

Trailers	S43*	S47*

1938 Tube Stock at Eastleigh:

DMs	10229‡	11229‡	
Trailers	012160‡	012272‡	012371‡

1938 Tube Stock at Strawberry Hill:

DMs	10139†	11172†	L148§	L149§			
NDMs	12027‡	12061†	12087§	12112‡			
Trailers	012211‡	012227‡	012259†	012292‡	012307‡	012364‡	012378‡

Notes *In Blue and grey livery
†In LUL bus red, white roundels
‡In LUL train red, cream window pillars
§In service stock livery (L148 maroon, L149 yellow)

London Transport Museum, Covent Garden, London.

The largest collection of preserved London Transport rolling stock is owned by London Transport itself. Most of the collection is now housed at the LT Museum at Covent Garden, which opened to the public on 29th March 1980.

Metropolitan Railway class A 4-4-0T steam locomotive No. 23, built 1866 by Beyer Peacock, later becoming service stock locomotive L45. This loco was withdrawn in 1948, following which it was restored to 1903 condition and eventually displayed at the Museum of British Transport at Clapham until its closure in 1972. It also appeared at the Underground Centenary celebrations at Neasden in May 1963.

Brill Branch (Wotton Tramway) 0-4-0T steam locomotive No. 807, built in 1872 by Aveling & Porter.

Metropolitan Railway 'Jubilee' steam stock coach, number unknown, dating from between 1887 and 1893 and built by Cravens Ltd, Sheffield. This car is currently in Ealing Common depot and is eventually to be restored for display in the LT Museum.

City & South London Railway loco-hauled 'padded-cell' coach No. 30 built by the Ashbury Carriage & Iron Co about 1890. This coach was displayed at the York Railway Museum from 1938 until closed in 1973.

City & South London Railway electric locomotive No.13 dating from about 1890. This locomotive was originally in the Science Museum, London, as No.1, but was transferred to the LT Museum in 1990 to celebrate the centenary of the City & South London Railway.

Metropolitan Railway milk van No. 3, built 1896 by Birmingham. This was converted to a breakdown van by the LPTB and renumbered BDV700. It was restored to original condition for the Underground Centenary in May 1963.

Metropolitan Railway steam stock 2nd class coach No. 400 dating from 1900 and built by the Met. at their Neasden Works. It was converted from steam stock to electric in 1921 as a 3rd Class Control Trailer, renumbered 6703 by the LPTB, and reconverted to steam stock for push-pull working on the Chalfont/Chesham shuttle in 1940, when it was further renumbered 519. It was stored at Clay Cross after withdrawal in 1962 and later at Preston Park, Brighton. In July 1976 the coach was taken to Ruislip depot for restoration, where work was completed during 1978.

Great Northern, Piccadilly & Brompton Railway tube motor coach No. 51 dating from 1909 and built by the Hungarian Railway Carriage & Machinery Works, Raab. The coach was renumbered 128 by the LER in 1926 and converted to a Ballast motor car No. L16 in the service stock fleet in 1929. Only the rear end of the car, back to the first window, is preserved, primarily to show the 'gate' arrangement.

City & South London Railway four-wheel wagon No. 63. This was one of a batch of 102 four-wheel wagons ordered from Gloucester in 1921 for the rebuilding of the City & South London Railway, and the majority were disposed of after the rebuilding was completed. This wagon has been laying derelict in London Road depot for many years and has now been acquired by the LT Museum for eventual restoration and display.

Metropolitan Railway electric locomotive No. 5 built by Metropolitan Vickers in 1922. It was named John Hampden in 1927.

London Transport Q23 stock driving motor car 4248. It was originally District Railway G class motor coach No. 644 and built by Gloucester in 1923. It was renumbered 238 in 1928 and 4148 in 1933. It was renumbered 4248 in 1965 to avoid the duplication of car numbers with 1967 tube stock. All G class cars were delivered with hand-operated passenger doors, being converted to air-door operation between 1938 and 1940.

London Transport 1938 tube stock motor car No. 11149 (cab end only) built by Metro-Cammell. This is used to demonstrate the operation of PCM equipment which is mounted adjacent to the cab end for visitors to see.

London Transport 1938 tube stock motor car No. 11182 built by Metro-Cammell. This car is restored in train red livery with gold transfers and passenger door control push buttons.

The LT Museum took delivery of ex-Metropolitan Railway Ballast Wagon BW214 in June 1982, and it is currently in store. This is one of two four-wheeled wagons of 1897 origin.

The cab of CP stock DM 54235 has been converted into a simulator. R49 aluminium-bodied DM car 22679 is also to be preserved, currently being stored in Ealing Common depot.

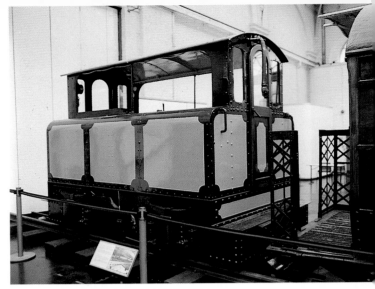

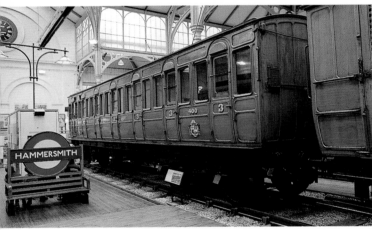

Above **C&SLR locomotive No.13 as repainted for the Centenary Exhibition in the LT Museum.** R.J. Greenaway

Metropolitan Railway 2nd Class steam stock coach No.400 dates from 1900, when it was built at the railway's Neasden Works. Fully restored at Ruislip depot between 1976 and 1978, it is another of the items on display at the London Transport Museum. R.J. Greenaway

Next to No.400 can be found this Met milk van, built in 1896 and used for transporting milk from the numerous farms along the Metropolitan Railway's route until 1936, when the LPTB converted it to a breakdown van. It was restored in 1963. R.J. Greenaway

Once part of the Metropolitan District Railway's G Class, this 1923-built car later became designated Q23 stock. Introduced with hand-worked doors, it was converted to air door operation in the late 1930s.
R.J. Greenaway

Below
The two-car train of 1938 stock, comprising DMs 10177 and 11177 on the Alderney Railway in the Channel Islands. John Trafford

Alderney Railway Society, Channel Islands
1938 stock DMs 10177 and 11177. Formerly owned by the North Downs Railway, these two cars were transferred to their new owners in mid-1987.

Bluebell Railway, Sheffield Park, Sussex.

Metropolitan Railway steam stock coaches 368 (1st and 3rd class coach built 1899), 387 (3rd class brake coach built 1900), 394 (3rd class coach built 1900), and 412 (1st and 3rd class coach built 1900). 387 was built by Cravens Ltd, Sheffield and the other three by the Ashbury Railway Carriage & Iron Co. The four coaches have a varied history. No. 387 was converted to a 3rd class electric driving motor car in 1907 and became 2761 when owned by the LPTB. No. 394 was converted to a 3rd class control trailer in 1921, becoming No. 6702 with the LPTB. Nos. 368 and 412 were converted to 1st class electric trailers in 1906 and became 9702 and 9705 respectively in LPTB ownership. The four cars were reconverted in 1940 to steam stock for push-pull working on the Chalfont/Chesham shuttle and were further renumbered 512 (2761), 515 (9702), 516 (9705) and 518 (6702).

The four coaches have been out of service for some time.

Metropolitan Railway ballast wagon BW4 of 1897 origin, transferred from Neasden depot in June 1982.

Four-wheel hopper wagons HW402 and HW433, built 1935 and 1951 respectively by Gloucester.

Buckinghamshire Railway Centre, Quainton Road, Quainton, Bucks

Metropolitan Railway class E 0-4-4T steam locomotive No. 1 dating from 1898, renumbered L44 in the service stock fleet by the LPTB in 1938.

London Transport service stock locomotive L99, originally GWR 0-6-0PT loco No. 7715 dating from 1930.

CP stock DM 54233. This car was moved to Quainton Road in October 1981 for preservation. After bomb damage during the second world war this car was rebuilt using part of Q38 trailer 013167, which had also suffered bomb damage.

In addition, two other cars of similar stock were taken by road from Ruislip depot at the end of June 1984. These were CO DM 52028 and COP trailer 013063. This therefore, makes a complete three-car unit.

Hurst Nelson brake van B557 was acquired by the Society on the same date as the CP stock car mentioned above.

Five-ton hand-operated crane C619, built in 1914 by Cowan Sheldon, and jib carrier J690. This latter vehicle was unique in being the only rail vehicle to be owned jointly by the Metropolitan and Great Central. C619 and J690 were to be found in Harrow goods yard. They were withdrawn in 1955 but were not taken to Quainton until May 1970.

LT flat brake wagon FB578, converted in 1950 from four-wheeled flat wagon F327.

LT four-wheeled flat wagon F329, built by Gloucester.

Colne Valley Railway

Four-wheeled hopper wagon HW421 built 1951 by Gloucester.

R38 DM 22624.

Gloucester Railway Carriage & Wagon Company

District Railway G class motor coach No. 662, renumbered 274 in 1929 and 4184 in 1934, later becoming part of the Q23 stock. The car is not now fitted with compressors or traction motors, which is how Gloucester delivered the G class in 1923. Following the takeover of the Gloucester factory, the car is now stored pending preservation by Gloucester City Council.

Isle of Wight Steam Railway, Haven Street

Four-wheeled hopper wagons HW435 and HW437, built in 1965 by BR at Shildon.

Keighley & Worth Valley Railway, Yorkshire

Metropolitan Railway steam stock brake coach 427 (3rd class seven-compartment brake coach built as a 1st class control trailer in 1905), 465 (3rd class nine-compartment coach built 1920), 509 (1st class seven-compartment coach built 1923). The coaches were numbered 2 (465), 3 (509) and 4 (427), but 427 and 465 have been restored and bear their former numbers. No. 509 is also being restored, but will take longer due to its poorer condition.

London Transport service stock locomotive L89, originally GWR 0-6-0PT loco No. 5775 dating from 1929.

The Buckinghamshire Railway Centre at Quainton Road has a number of ex-London Transport vehicles in its collection. Included are: Three-car CO/CP stock unit (with DM 53028 nearest the camera); Flat Brake FB578; and four-car wheeled Flat Wagon F329.
Steve Ellingham

District Line R38 stock DM 22624 is preserved by the Colne Valley Railway and is seen at Chappell on 30th July 1989.
Steve Ellingham

Below A replica four-wheeled first class District Railway coach can be found on the Kent & East Sussex Railway.
Steve Ellingham

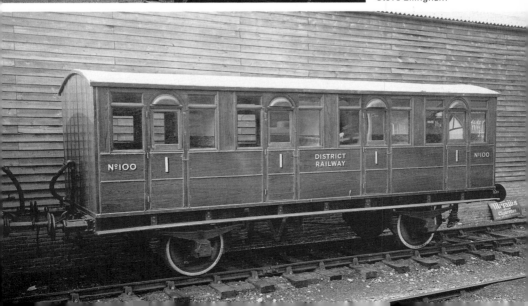

Kent & East Sussex Railway

In late 1979 and early 1980, restoration was carried out on a coach now numbered 100 as a 1st class 4-compartment steam stock car dating from around 1865. The coach body was retrieved in two halves which have been joined together and mounted on a modern underframe. Whilst the coach is thus very much a hybrid, it has been superbly restored and first saw passenger service again on 24th August 1980.

London Underground Railway Society

City & South London Railway loco-hauled coaches 135 (dating from 1902) and 163 (dating from 1907). These are currently stored at Ruislip depot.

District Line Q35 stock trailer No. 08063, formerly N class trailer (1st and 3rd class) No. 8063 built in 1935. It was renumbered in 1950 when converted to air-door operation and is currently at Ealing Common depot having been restored.

London Underground Railway Training Centre, Wood Lane, London W12

Parts of 1938 tube stock DM 11103 and 1935 stock trailer 012488 have been used in a 'mock-up' car now numbered '999' to teach trainee guards the operation of air doors and associated equipment. The two cars were damaged beyond repair in a collision at Tooting Broadway in 1962 and were reconstructed for their current use when the present Railway Training Centre was opened in 1963.

The London Underground Railway Society's Q35 trailer, coupled to the LT Museum's R49 DM car 22679 in Willesden yard, when on route to Ilford for the BR Open-day in May 1989. R.J. Greenaway

The two C&SLR coach bodies belonging to the London Underground Railway Society are located at Ruislip on LUL wagons. Car 135 is seen being loaded onto RW824 on 22 May 1990. R.J. Greenaway

Five cars of pre-1938 stock on the Isle of Wight returned to the mainland in early October 1990 for possible restoration to service. Two cars (27 and 44) were repainted back into Underground colours before shipping — 27 is seen at Ryde St John's Road on 2nd October 1990. R.J. Greenaway

Seen at Fishbourne on 3rd October 1990, car 27 has been painted into 1920s livery, complete with maroon doors. R.J. Greenaway

On the Fishbourne-Portsmouth vehicle ferry on 3rd October 1990, bound for Fratton, Cammell Laird trailer 44 has been painted in 1930s livery. R.J. Greenaway

Museum of London
Steam crane C621, built by Thomas Smith & Sons, 1935, secondhand ex-McAlpine in 1958. Currently stored.

North Downs Railway, Dartford, Kent
Former T stock DMs 2758 and 2749 (latterly ESL118A/B). Hurst Nelson brake van B560 of 1935 (this replaced B556, which was damaged by fire).

North Norfolk Railway, Sheringham
Four-wheeled hopper wagons HW426 and HW429, built in 1951 by Gloucester.

Passmore Edwards Museum
Metropolitan Railway 1904 coach, acquired in 1985 from the Army at Shoeburyness. Confirmation is sought that this car is 3rd class trailer 9486.

CP stock DM 54256, moved from Ruislip depot by road in November 1982.

Science Museum, Kensington, London SW7
London Transport pre-1938 tube stock driving motor car 3327, originally London Electric Railway tube motor coach No. 297 dating from 1927.

Former LT brake van B560 took the place of B556 on the North Downs Steam Railway, B556 having been damaged by fire. In addition to the brake van, the NDSR also have the two-car train of ex-LT 'T' stock, one car of which can be seen in the background. Steve Ellingham

Severn Valley Railway, Bridgnorth, Shropshire

London Transport service stock steam locomotive L95, originally GWR 0-6-0PT loco No. 5764 dating from 1929.

Four-wheeled hopper wagons HW410, HW411 (1938 Gloucester) and HW436 (1965 BR Shildon), also Lining Machine PTL764.

Southern Steam Trust, Swanage

Plasser Theurer VKR05 Tamping Machine PBT762, built in 1966.

Standard Gauge Steam Trust, Tyeseley, West Midlands

London Transport service stock steam locomotive L90, origiunally GWR 0-6-0PT loco No. 7760 dating from 1930.

London Transport service stock steam locomotive L94, originally GWR 0-6-0PT loco No. 7752 dating from 1930.

Worcester Locomotive Society, Hereford

London Transport service stock steam locomotive L92, originally GWR 0-6-0PT loco No. 5786 dating from 1927.

An unidentified ex-LT hopper wagon shunts at Buckfastleigh on the Dart Valley Railway in Devon.
Steve Ellingham

APPENDIX

CAR RENUMBERINGS

For various reasons some of the rolling stock in use on the Underground has been renumbered since new. This appendix gives details of all renumberings of current stock. For the causes of the changes please refer to the appropriate chapters.

A60/62 STOCK

Original No.	Renumbered	Date
5028	**5232**	6.85
6028	**6232**	6.85
6117	**6233**	8.85
5117	**5233**	8.85
5008	**5034**	7.85

1956 TUBE STOCK

Original No.	Renumbered	Date	Original No.	Renumbered	Date
40000	**1000**	3.65	42001	**1006**	10.65
45000	**2000**	3.65	45003	**2006**	10.65
44000	**9001**	3.65	41001	**1007**	10.65
43000	**1001**	3.65	40002	**1008**	6.65
42000	**1002**	3.65	45004	**2008**	6.65
45001	**2002**	3.65	44002	**9009**	6.65
41000	**1003**	3.65	43002	**1009**	6.65
40001	**1004**	3.65	42002	**1010**	3.65
45002	**2004**	3.65	45005	**2010**	3.65
44001	**9005**	3.65	41002	**1011**	3.65
43001	**1005**	3.65			

1960 TUBE STOCK

Original No.	Renumbered	Date	Renumbered	Date	Renumbered	Date
012366			**4921**	2.78		
012229			**4927**	4.77		
092392	A92392	2.44	012392	10.50	**4929**	2.76

1959 TUBE STOCK

Original No.	Renumbered	Date	Renumbered	Date
1070	**1309R**	8.77		
1085	1031R	5.88	**1031**	6.90

1962 TUBE STOCK

Original No.	Renumbered	Date	Original No.	Renumbered	Date
2408	2448	5.83	2644	2720	2.83
2448	2462	7.83	2648	2732*	5.83
2452	2522	8.83	2650	2590	7.83
2460	2490	6.83	2674	2702	9.82
2462	2478	7.83	2678	2600	6.82
2474	2494	6.83	2682	2650	3.83
2478	2488	5.83	2684	2648	4.83
2488	2460	4.83	2692	2684	4.83
2490	2492	8.83	2694	2718	6.83
2492	2504	7.83	2696	2704	10.83
2494	2452	5.83	2700	2644	12.82
2500	2510	6.83	2702	2612	9.82
2504	2474	7.83	2704	2408	8.83
2510	2570	7.83	2714	2582	8.83
2518	2602	7.83	2718	2734	4.82
2522	2524	7.83	2720	2638	2.83
2524	2528	10.83	2728	2682	7.83
2528	2500	7.83	2732	2714	6.83
2532	2618	4.83	2734	2678	5.82
2570	2518	4.83	9459	9501	12.84
2580	2728	6.83	1459	1501	12.84
2582	2696	9.83	9501	9459	5.89
2600	2674	8.82	1501	1459	5.89
2602	2532	6.83	9657	9741	6.84
2608	2692	3.83	9741	9657	6.84
2612	2624	10.82	1659	1531	1.87
2618	2580	7.83	9659	9751	7.89
2624	2632	10.82	1531	1416	2.90
2628	2700	11.82	1732	1542	9.90
2632	2628	11.82	9747	9543	9.90
2638	2608	2.83			

*2732 was further renumbered 2542 in 9.90

1967 TUBE STOCK

Original No.	To Acton	Renumbered	Ex-Acton	Re-Entered Service
4101	6.88	4180	7.88	7.88
3101	6.88	3180	7.88	7.88
4103	7.88	4181	2.89	4.89
3103	7.88	3181	2.89	4.89
4105	7.88	4182	7.88	8.88
3105	7.88	4182	7.88	8.88
4107	6.88	4183	2.89	3.89
3107	6.88	3183	2.89	3.89
4122	6.88	4186	7.88	12.88
3122	6.88	3186	7.88	12.88
4141	9.87	4184	10.87	12.87
3141	9.87	3184	10.87	12.87
4152	4.88	4185	5.88	6.88
3152	4.88	3185	5.88	6.88

CAR RENUMBERINGS

1972 TUBE STOCK

Cars	To Acton	Renumbered	Ex-Acton	Re-Entered Service
3216	4.88	**3085**	5.88	6.88
4216	4.88	**4085**	5.88	6.88
4316	4.88	**4152**	6.88	7.88
3316	4.88	**3152**	6.88	7.88
3217	5.88	**3080**	7.88	7.88
4217	5.88	**4080**	7.88	7.88
4317	5.88	**4101**	6.88	7.88
3317	5.88	**3101**	6.88	7.88
3220	4.88	**3086**	7.88	12.88
4220	9.86	**4086**	7.88	12.88
4320	9.86	**4122**	7.88	9.88
3320	6.88	**3122**	7.88	9.88
3223	6.88	**3082**	7.88	8.88
4223	6.88	**4082**	7.88	8.88
4323	6.88	**4103**	8.88	12.88
3323	6.88	**3103**	8.88	12.88
3225	7.88	**3083**	2.89	3.89
4225	7.88	**4083**	2.89	3.89
4325	7.88	**4107**	2.89	3.89
3325	7.88	**3107**	2.89	3.89
4516	4.88	**4141**	6.88	7.88
3516	4.88	**3141**	6.88	7.88
4520	6.87	**4084***	10.87	12.87
3520	6.87	**3084***	10.87	12.87
4527	7.88	**4081***	2.89	4.89
3527	7.88	**3081***	2.89	4.89
4529	6.88	**4105**	2.89	6.89
3529	6.88	**3105**	2.89	6.89

*Also converted from 'D' end to 'A' end

ABBREVIATIONS USED FOR CARBUILDERS

Birmingham Birmingham Railway Carriage & Wagon Company Ltd.
Cravens Cravens Ltd, Sheffield.
Gloucester Gloucester Railway Carriage & Wagon Company Ltd.
Metro-Cammell* Metropolitan-Cammell Carriage & Wagon Co Ltd, Birmingham.
BREL BREL Ltd, Derby (formerly British Rail Engineering Ltd).
Pickering R. Y. Pickering & Co, Wishaw, Lanarkshire, Scotland.
Derby BR Workshops, Derby.

*Formerly Metropolitan Carriage, Wagon & Finance Company Ltd, shown in lists as Metro-Carriage.